Extraordinary Adventures
of an
Ordinary Man

J. Merrill Rosenberger

Order this book online at www.trafford.com
or email orders@trafford.com

Most Trafford titles are also available at major online book retailers.

Printed in the United States of America.

ISBN: 978-1-4907-1845-3 (sc)
ISBN: 978-1-4907-1847-7 (hc)
ISBN: 978-1-4907-1846-0 (e)

Library of Congress Control Number: 2013919521

Trafford rev. 10/29/2013

www.trafford.com
North America & international
toll-free: 1 888 232 4444 (USA & Canada)
fax: 812 355 4082

This book I dedicate to my younger brother Harold whose life was cut short by cancer on March 25th, 2005. We shared many of the same experiences during my time in Red Lake and the memories will live on.

CHAPTER 1

The "Hike"—the early days in Red Lake

The fall of the year 1956 found us in Red Lake, Ontario, Canada for our first winter in the bush. I was 16 years old at the time and my father was an airplane owner and pilot. He always wished to be a commercial airline pilot and although he was a talented and very experienced pilot he lacked the education that commercial airlines required of their pilots. As a result, when an opportunity presented itself, for him to become a bush pilot he could not refuse the chance to pursue his dream. Although I never wanted to leave Pennsylvania there was a degree of adventure that drew me towards the idea of living in the northland. I had no idea of what I was going to experience but was looking forward to the adventure anyway.

We had arrived in Red Lake several weeks earlier and moved into our new cabin. This was going to be a completely different experience for me as there were no toilet facilities in the cabin! No running hot water and the only water available

1

to us was pumped by hand in the kitchen sink from a well that had been dug by hand near the kitchen. The cabin was designed for the climate we were going to experience as the center of the house was the living room. In that room was a coal oil stove that was intended to heat the entire house but rarely did when the temperatures dropped below minus 30 degrees. There were three bedrooms, one on the southwest corner of the cabin one on the northwest corner of the cabin and one on the northeast corner. The kitchen was on the south east corner and our kitchen door opened into the unheated garage where my father's 1954 Chevrolet sedan was kept when not being used. It was always plugged into electric outlets to heat the rod that was drilled and mounted into the oil pan to keep the oil from forming a solid thick mass of very viscous material which would make impossible the ability to turn the engine over for starting on the very cold days.

I shared the bedroom on the northwest corner of the cabin with my younger brother Harold who was 12 years old at the time. The corner of the bedroom had a window on both sides of the corner and there was a desk built in that corner for me to do my homework. I was soon to learn the cold winter weather would build an ice barrier on the inside of the window pane about an inch thick. It would remain that way until spring, still allowing light to enter the room but no ability to see through it. It was not unusual to wake in the morning with a pile of frost on our pillows from the steam of our breath as we slept. Our beds were made of freshly cut lumber with no springs and a full size mattress was placed on the wooden lower bunk as well as the upper bunk. Harold and I both slept in the lower bunk to share our body heat.

Bob and Phil slept in their bunk in the third bedroom. Mother and dad slept in the southwest corner bedroom.

During the day all the bedroom doors would be closed so that the oil stove in the living room could heat the living area and kitchen as mother and Phil (who was not yet in school at 5 years of age) were the only ones left at home. At night our bedroom doors were allowed to be open a few inches to allow a minimum amount of heat in and still maintain a reasonably warm living room and kitchen for the following morning.

I walked three miles each way to high school each day which kept my young body in great physical condition. The winter temperatures varied from 20 below zero to 52 below zero and that walk was sometimes a very uncomfortable one. My younger brother Harold had a shorter walk to middle school which was in town. My brother Bob also had a shorter walk to elementary school which was also in town. Our cabin was located on the north side of Red Lake at the top of a rather high hill for that part of the north. My school was about 2 miles south of Red Lake in a rather desolate area in the bush although it was a new building and even had a rugby field complete with goal posts. Saturday nights were bath nights and mother would fill a huge bucket with ice cold water pumped from the well in the kitchen and she would heat the water on the stove. The family would gather in the kitchen as one by one each of us would bathe sitting on a wooden stool in front of the oil stove in the living room. Several weeks of bathing in this manner made us appreciate the beautiful white porcelain bath tub we had enjoyed in Pennsylvania, with both hot and cold running water to fill to any desired depth. It wasn't very long when the excitement of taking a bucket bath wore off.

One Saturday afternoon I asked mother if I could go for a hike. She said it was OK so of course Harold wanted to go too and when I agreed Bob wanted to go so then Phil said he wanted to go as well. So off the four of us went, on an adventure. I had a compass which was on a wrist strap that fit over your winter coat and although compass readings are not very accurate that far north it did give you a general idea where north was. We headed over the big rock behind our house and were on a NNW heading. It was a cold overcast fall day of late August or very early September. There was no snow on the ground and the leaves had already fallen off the Poplar, Aspens and Birch trees. We walked for close to an hour when I came across an old abandoned gold mine. It was a hole in the ground with a shaft that went straight down. There was a wood ladder that went down about 10 feet to a platform where another ladder went down from there to yet another platform. I had not brought any rope with me so I wasn't sure I wanted to venture down that hole with no rope for a safety device. In any case I decided to try putting some weight on the first wrung of the ladder. I hadn't even put half my weight on it when it gave way and fell hitting the first platform then falling to the second platform and we could hear the wrung bouncing off the walls of the shaft and platforms as it continued to fall. I realized how fortunate I was that I had not put my entire weight on that platform and fallen to my death because I know that Harold and my younger brothers could never have found their way back to Red Lake.

We were all so focused on the mine shaft that none of us noticed it had started to snow. We had been busy dropping big rocks down the mine shaft to see how deep the hole was. Time had gone by quickly and I would guess we had spent about two hours around that mine shaft. We were all laying on our belly's looking down this black hole. The passing of time finally dawned on me and I decided we should start back towards home. Was I ever surprised to see the ground was now white with snow and the dried leaves that we overturned which was my trail I was going to follow home was completely covered in snow. Here I was with my 3 younger brothers in tow and

4

nothing looked the same after it all turned white with snow. I took a compass reading and did a reverse azimuth calculation and headed off in that basic direction. I wasn't wearing a watch but I was pretty sure we walked about an hour before we found the mine shaft so I figured we had about an hour walk to get home. My heart was pounding as I thought about the consequences of being off course just one or two degrees either direction and we would miss Red Lake entirely!!!! The snow was coming down fast and furious and there was now about 4 inches on the ground. Nothing at all looked familiar and I kept turning backwards to look at my trail to make sure we were going in a straight line. Thank God for He was obviously watching over us as we stumbled through the wilderness and we arrived at a huge rock. We continued to climb and when we came to the edge, I was looking down on the roof of our house. Do you realize how unlikely that scenario was? The chances of that happening are nearly impossible. Yet it is true and the four of us are witness to the fact that God was looking after us. I have never forgotten that experience and never will.

CHAPTER 2

Wolf encounter!

O ne of the more fun things I enjoyed doing living in Red Lake was calling wolves at night. Even on a night when it was totally quiet and still, if you were to howl like a wolf you were almost always answered with the cries of multiple wolves. Sometimes they were fairly close to our cabin and sometimes they were quite a distance away. The one thing about wolves however is they could be 20 feet away from you but you would more than likely never see them. They are so skilled at not being seen. I am convinced that on more than one occasion I have called a wolf or wolves to within bow range but never caught sight of them although they were certainly observing me. Timber wolves are huge animals! Some big males shot by bush pilots weighed well over 200 pounds and I have seen wolf prints in the snow or mud that would fill most of a saucer under a coffee cup.

It was a clear cold winter day and I was walking home from down town Red Lake.

For what reason I was in town I do not recall but I was taking the "long way" home to go past a certain girl's house that I knew. Our cabin was up on a hill out of and past the Village of Red Lake. Having walked about three miles to school every day for the entire school year had me in excellent physical condition. Every road in Red Lake in those days was a dirt road. The down town area had wooden sidewalks to walk on in the spring because the road would turn very muddy when the ground began to thaw. In 1956/57 the downtown area was about 400 yards long. There was board walk on both sides of the road and there were boot cleaners to clean your boots before entering the stores. There were not that many stores in those days either. There was a hotel, two bars, a restaurant, grocery store, a Hudson Bay store, a barber shop, a jewelry store, a hardware store and a Post office. That was about all there were in the early days. When walking west, past the last store in town the boardwalk stopped and from then on you walked on the snow or the dirt and mud. I was walking west out of town so I was walking on the frozen ice/snow covered road. To be able to pass this certain girls house I had to walk about a quarter mile past down town and then make a right turn and head on up the hill another 1/3 mile to our cabin. Since there was no road in that area I had to go through some deep snow if it had not crusted enough for me to walk on top of it. When young and with the age of puberty coursing through your veins deep snow was a minor issue. I had nearly came to my friend's house when I looked up to see a wolf bearing down on me at a full run. He was about 50 yards away but he was really covering the ground. I could clearly see his tongue and his fangs as he sped towards me. My heart skipped a beat and started thumping and I knew it was my end! I stopped walking and froze in position waiting for the impact of the attack. You will never know the chill that goes through you like a stream of ice when faced with inevitable death! I threw my parka over my head and took both hands and put them close to my neck where I felt he would sink his fangs. I would not die easily of that I was sure. At the moment of impact I braced myself and held my breath! Nothing happened!!! He was no longer in front of me so I spun around to see him chasing the panel truck of the service station owner. Little did I know then, but that owner (several years prior) had taken their huge Malamute female dog which was coming into heat, out into the bush along with 25 pounds of frozen fish and caribou meat and tied her to a tree. One of two things will happen in a situation like that. A wolf will smell the female in heat and come and breed her or he will smell the female in heat and come and kill her. In this case the wolf bred the female and she gave birth to this huge wolf dog puppy which the owner raised. These animals are not rare as it turns out, but fairly common in the northland. They are extremely loyal to their master but have been known to be vicious towards strangers. In my case the loyalty of this wolf dog to his master was greater than his viciousness towards me and I was very lucky. I had seen before and saw afterwards many wolves and he looked a whole lot more like a wolf than a dog I assure you. I saw that wolf dog several times after that but he never paid any attention to me and I did not complain about that. How I wished I had a wolf dog at that stage of my life. It was not to be.

CHAPTER 3

Moose Hunting with Cowboy Pete

One of the first friends I made after arriving in Red Lake was an Indian named "Cowboy Pete". He was an unusual person to say the least. He spoke fairly good English as well as fluent Ojibwa and unlike the average full blooded Ojibwa Indian, Cowboy Pete was a strikingly good looking man. He had steel grey eyes that looked as though they could burn a hole through you when he looked at you and he never wasted words on small talk. When he spoke I listened.

Cowboy Pete and I were on a moose hunt. I had purchased a half dozen broad head arrow tips through a mail order, for my wood arrows and was going to attempt to shoot a moose with my long bow. I was excited because I was with Cowboy Pete and he thought it was neat that I was going to use a bow to shoot a moose and he was going to back me up with a rifle.

We moved silently through the bush and being spring time most of the snow had disappeared. There still were patches of snow here and there but generally speaking the spring time was in full swing. We saw the occasional ptarmigan. They were changing into their summer plumage but were still half white and half brown in color with their tufted ankles of all white. I would have loved to shoot one with the bow but didn't want to waste a broad head with the chance I might lose it or damage it. I may need all of the arrows I had with me for the moose. Neither did Pete want to shoot a bird with his 308 caliber rifle as it would have obliterated the tiny bird. So all we could do was to watch them and wish as we walked on. Along with the 308 caliber rifle that Pete was carrying he also had strapped to his hip a 22 caliber revolver with 22 longs as his ammunition. We had seen some bear tracks and once we thought we smelled the bear but never did see him.

We were skirting a small lake when we suddenly came across what appeared to be a very angry beaver. He was sitting straight up and grinding his huge long teeth at us. We could see his island fortress some distance from shore and we were not blocking his escape to it. Never the less it appeared he had other plans and they did not include escaping from Pete and me. Instead he had decided to challenge us to a fight as he began coming towards us walking on his hind legs and still gnawing his teeth. I had never seen such a brazen beaver in my life. Usually they make a break for the water and with a quick slap of their tail they are gone. Not this big guy! He was mad and he was intent on showing us who was boss! He kept hobbling towards us on his hind feet and when he was about ten feet away Cowboy Pete reached for his revolver and took careful aim right at the beaver's nose. The pistol cracked and the beaver shook his head and kept coming. Blood was now running from his nose and yet he was still moving forward! I had side stepped and was now out of the beaver's way but the beaver was heading right for Pete. Pete aimed again and squeezed off another shot. This time the beaver dropped and it was not long when he expired and was not going to challenge anyone again. The second bullet had hit him in the eye and entered his brain. Cowboy Pete himself was surprised at the tenacity of that beaver and told me he never had a beaver come after him like that one did. Both Pete and I carried hatchets and knives on our belt and Pete began chopping a dead fall tree and soon had lots of firewood. He gathered kindling and soon had a roaring fire going. After skinning the beaver he cut a hind quarter off and part of the fatty tail, impaling it with a green willow branch. He had sharpened both ends of the inch thick willow branch and after spearing the beaver hind Quarter and piece of beaver tail on one end, he stuck the other end into the ground with the meat close to the fire. About an hour later we were eating some of the sweetest, best tasting meat I have ever enjoyed. That was my first meal of fresh beaver and I am sorry to say it has been my last, even to this day.

We hunted all day and just before dusk at about 10:30 PM we headed back towards Red Lake and home. We never did see a moose that day.

That night I lay outside on my back on the cool ground watching the light spectacle as the "northern lights" displayed across the arctic sky. It kept me entertained for hours! You really have not lived if you have never had the opportunity to see that beautiful display of Gods Handiwork and to hear the distant cry of the wolf. What a wonderful, experience and I thank the Lord in heaven for allowing me to witness unbelievable spectacular displays of Gods wonders.

CHAPTER 4

Pikangikum, Ontario

I n 1954, before my dad moved us to Red Lake there were two young pioneers that I must write about. These two young men were from Pennsylvania and lived comfortable lives with modern conveniences prior to their move to Northwestern Ontario. They had volunteered to devote their young lives to the religious calling of the northland. It was indeed my greatest honor to have known these two men!

Their names are Johnny Stoltzfus and Ralph Halteman.

They were both handy around carpentry as well as basic survival and Irvan Schantz, the founder of Northern Lights Gospel Mission agreed to fly them into a desolate isolated place called Pikangikum. They took with them basic survival equipment such as rifle, ammo, tent, sleeping bags, hatchet, matches etc. Pikangikum is located about 200 miles NNW of Red Lake and the only way there was by plane.

They set out soon after arriving there to collect food and soon were able to harvest a nice fat moose. After skinning and cleaning the animal and cooking a good meal they dug a deep depression into the earth, wrapped the meat in cheese cloth inside a canvas outer wrap and buried it to keep it cool. They also took some of the meat and smoked it to preserve it.

This is the way their adventure in Pikangikum began. Several days later Irvan Shantz returned with his plane and dropped off a portable saw mill.

With that Johnny and Ralph began the long hard battle of clearing some land and cutting the timber into workable lumber. Over the following weeks Irvan flew in regularly to re-supply their staples such as canned vegetables, flour and coffee. He also brought bags of cement and nails for building. Not having time to dry the lumber properly they mixed the cement, poured the foundation and began building a cabin to live in. As the cabin began taking shape Irvan again flew into Pikangikum, this time bringing a wood stove for the cabin along with lengths of stove pipe complete with a "Charlie Noble". By this time the cabin was nearly finished so the building of a refrigerated and elevated shed for fresh meat was begun. There was more than enough saw dust from the saw mill to use as insulation and as fall approached and the lake began freezing over it was time for collecting fire wood for the winter. Once the ice on the lake reached about 18 inches in thickness they took a saw and cut large squares of ice for the refrigerator. After laying about 12 inches of saw dust down on the floor of the ice shed they carefully laid their precious frozen meat wrapped in cheese cloth and canvas and covered the contents with another 12 inches of saw dust.

One day as Johnny and Ralph were out hunting for deer they found themselves trapped by a winter blizzard. They had not planned on being gone overnight so they were not prepared for what happened next. The snow was coming down fast and furious and they were facing a whiteout situation. As darkness was fast approaching and the temperature was dropping they headed for a nearby lake. By the time they arrived at the lake the snow had stopped falling but the temperature was now in the area of 40 degrees below zero! They found a flat area near the shore and the two of them began hauling dead wood and windfalls to that flat area. With some heavy tree bark they cleared a large area of all the snow and piled the logs and windfalls in a crisscross pattern. Before long they had a giant bonfire blazing away on the sandy shores of the lake. The flames reaching as high as 20 feet in the air and as the fire waned they absorbed the heat and watched as northern lights danced across the sky. Finally with the fire now out they scraped the hot ashes off the cleared area and they slept on the hot sand in comfort till morning! This experience was told to me by Johnny just before I left home for the last time and went back to the good old USA.

CHAPTER 5

Fishing Paradise!

From my very youngest memories I have always loved fishing. I had an old fishing rod and reel along with a small tackle box with various lures, plugs and spoons. When we arrived in Red Lake in 1956 however, I discovered my fishing equipment had not made the trip. How very disappointing!

I learned there was a sporting goods store in Red Lake so the first weekend there I went in search of the store. All the roads in Red Lake were dirt roads and there was a main road that paralleled the shoreline of Red Lake. All the stores in town were on that main road. At the far end of the town of Red Lake the road stopped. I knew if there really was a sporting goods store it would be on that main road. I finally found it and it was in a hardware store combined with all the hardware.

I purchased a nice rod and reel, several spoons, a few plugs and a couple of spinners. One of the spoons I purchased was a red and white stripped spoon called a "dare devil". As it turned out I could have saved some hard earned cash by just buying one spoon and that one being the red and white stripped "Dare Devil".

On my first fishing expedition which was a small lake near our cabin I managed to wade through the reeds and cat tails to where I could finally cast my red and white spoon. To my great surprise the spoon had no sooner hit the water and it was struck by something big! The fight was on! I had 10 pound test fishing line and whatever was on my hook was straining that line to the limit! I would fight that fish and every time I got him close he would make a "bee line" for parts unknown and the struggle continued. After a 30 minute bout I finally was able to land the fish and it was a 20 pound Northern Pike. It was exciting!

I put him on a stringer and continued to fish and soon caught several smaller fish called Pickrel. They may have averaged 2 to 3 pounds each. I added them to my stringer and began my proud walk back to our cabin with my prize catch. That night we had fresh Northern Pike for dinner and it was good. A little bony but still the taste was really good. Mother was an excellent cook.

The following day I spoke with my friend Chris Schantz and told him about my good luck fishing. He did not seem to share my excitement but implied that fishing was much better in some coves he knew about on Red Lake. I talked him into taking me fishing to his favorite fishing holes.

The first thing I noticed was that Chris did not even have a tackle box. He had a rod and reel and a red and white Dare Devil tied to the end of his line. When I mentioned that he did not even have a tackle box and what kind of fisherman has no tackle box he said "why waste your money, all you need is a dare devil to catch fish here". Soon we were in one of his secret coves he had talked about so proudly. He dropped the stone anchor and we began fishing. On my third cast I thought I had snagged the bottom when suddenly the "bottom" started fighting back!!! This fish felt different then the Northern Pike

I had caught before and it seemed to me this fish was bigger. I don't remember how long the fight lasted but when I finally hauled the fish over the side and into the boat it was a Walleye. What a fight he put up!!! He weighed 16 pounds but pound for pound he put up a bigger fight then the Northern Pike.

Chris caught several Walleye and a couple Pike and along with my Walleye and Pike we both had dinner for the families that night.

The next time we went fishing Chris told me we were going to a new location that would take an hour or more to get to. So, off we went with his 14 foot boat and 15 HP outboard motor. We were in Red Lake but Red Lake is a very large lake that went on for miles and miles, winding its way around twists and turns with many islands along the way.

Chris slowed the boat down to an idle and threw a large metal bucket over the side. The bucket was tied to a metal eyelet on the back of the boat and the bucket had several small holes in the bottom and sides. He called it a floating anchor and it slowed our boat down considerably. I watched as he dropped his red and white dare devil into the water and slowly fed the line out as we trolled along at a fairly slow speed. I followed the same procedure and before long we both had fish on our lines. This fish was obviously much bigger than anything I had ever caught before and it was testing my equipment. I was sure my line would break and if not my line then my rod would break in two. We both fought our fish for more than an hour and were actually getting arm weary when we finally were able to pull these lunker fish aside the boat. We had each caught very large Lake Trout that weighed in the area of 30 to 35 pounds. These fish had never seen a lure or spoon before and would strike at anything that moved in the water. I now understood why Chris said he did not need a tackle box.

CHAPTER 6

Flight with a crazy man!

My first winter in Red Lake was a real learning experience. I not only met a lot of new school students I also met a few legendary residents and part time residents.

One of those part time residents was a young fellow named Jimmy Lendooken. Jimmy was a half breed Indian. His father was an Ojibwa Indian named Turtle Head Moose and his mother's name was Heather Lendooken. She kept her maiden name and gave it to her son Jimmy. Jimmy was two years older than me at 18 years of age and he was an experienced bush plane pilot with a reputation as being a bit on the dare devil side if not plain crazy.

Every spring there was a bet in place of $50.00 for the last plane off the ice before breakup. Jimmy, living up to his reputation was the winner for the last three years. The fourth year he not only lost his bet he nearly lost his plane as well. It partially broke through the ice and was saved only by a tripod device that spread the weight of the plane over a larger portion of the ice. It was then dragged to shore on the skis of the tripod.

Before that happened however I was down by the ice covered lake one Saturday morning and his plane was loaded to the ceiling with furs from trapper John. He saw me walking past and asked me if I wanted to ride with him to the fur depot to drop off his furs. I might mention that a bush plane has only one seat and that is the seat the pilot sits in. All the rest of the space inside the aircraft is for freight. Being young and "immortal" I excitedly said "sure thing but where am I going to sit"? He responded that I would be lying on top of the furs. With him pressing down on the stack of furs and me scrambling my best I was able to climb on top of the shaky load of furs. My back was against the ceiling of the plane and my belly was on the furs. It was a tight fit. After warming the engine a bit and taxiing out to the center of the lake we took off to the east. Once we reached an altitude of about 2500 feet we turned west and headed for the fur trader about a 20 minute flight away. Jimmy was singing all the way at the top of his lungs!!! Then I heard him yell "FUR TRADERS HERE WE COME" and we went into a dive. We were going straight down and I was sure we were going to crash. I yelled at him to pull up but he just kept laughing! Then at what must have been the last second he pulled back on the yoke and the g-force of the pull out squashed the furs far enough that I could for the first time see out the wind shield. (the furs were compressed at least 12 or 14 inches). I saw the snow covered ice coming up to meet us very fast and jimmy was still laughing! Suddenly we hit the snow covered ice and we hit it hard. It nearly knocked the wind out of me. The plane must have bounced 30 feet off the lake and we hit the snow again. Jimmy was still laughing and screaming "ride em' cowboy"! The plane finally settled down on the ice and we sped along towards the dock to unload the furs. As soon as I was able to climb out of the plane I felt like I had to kiss the ground as I was never so happy to be alive as I was then. It was then I heard the sound. It was a sound I have never heard before or since. The sound kept going and going for almost 10 minutes! When one of the sled drivers came close enough I asked him what that noise was. He responded, "that is the noise Jimmy makes when he lands here showing off"!!!! What the noise was is the sound the ice makes when it is about 5 feet thick and it is impacted with a heavy loaded aircraft that causes a wave action under the ice. That sound is the sound of ice cracking all across the lake due to the wave action from the impact.

I walked back to Red Lake from there and got home that evening. I never rode with Jimmy Lendooken again.

Post Script: Sad note!

In 1958 after I had returned to Pennsylvania I received a letter from my mother explaining how Jimmy had begun drinking. He had flown to Winnipeg, Manatoba to change his plane from ski's to pontoons for flying in the summer time. On a clear day he took off from Winnipeg heading for Red Lake. According to his flight plan he was to arrive at Red Lake 2 hours 15 minutes later. 8 hours later a search party was sent out to look for his aircraft. Soon all the bush pilots in the area were looking for Jimmy's Cessna 180 airplane. A week had gone by but no sign of jimmy or his plane. About two weeks after the first letter about Jimmy's drinking I received another letter from mother. They found the remains of Jimmy's plane which had crashed about half way during his flight back home.

There were empty and broken booze bottles found at the crash site and mother explained that what the wolves had not eaten of Jimmy Lendooken was placed in a plastic bag and brought home for burial. He would have been 20 years old at the time of his death.

CHAPTER 7

An Indian funeral

C hris Schantz was the son of Irvan Schantz, the founder
of "Northern Lights Gospel Mission". He was my age
and we were close friends.

One day Chris came by and asked me if I wanted to go to
an Indian funeral. Having nothing better to do I said sure so
I jumped into the front seat of his 1946 Ford sedan and away
we went. We drove toward Balmertown for a ways and then
parked the car next to a stream of water. From there we began
a very long walk down a well used trail. We must have walked
several miles when we arrived at this Indian village. It was
not what one would think an Indian village would look like
at all. There were no teepee's or picturesque campfires. The
buildings were made of cardboard and canvas and there were
boughs lying on the roof to keep the rain out. It was early
summer. All the shacks had a very low doorway that even I
had to stoop down to go inside. Chris spoke Ojibwa, at least
enough to get by and we met an elder and Chris told him in
his language that we were there to pay respects to the tribe
by honoring their funeral process. He led us to a doorway

of one of the shacks and I could smell something dead and decaying as we entered. There was a soft mournful song being sung by a half dozen or so Indian women as they sat in a semi circle and they were rocking in unison back and forth with their singing. One of the women near the center of the group was cuddling an infant wrapped in moss and covered with a torn piece of canvas. There was a young man inside that directed us to squat down as were the women sitting on the floor. We sat down Indian style. Although we did not sing along we did sway back and forth with the women. The smell was horrible and I wanted to throw up, but I didn't. When the women stopped singing one of the women spoke to Chris in Ojibwa. She spoke for about 15 minutes and was motioning with her hands all through her speaking. When she finished she began crying and was joined by the other women as they all cried together. The young man ushered Chris and I out of the very dark and smelly shack into the fresh air and I was never happier to be outside. Chris was wiping tears from his eyes and when I asked him what was wrong, this is what he told me the Indian woman said to him as we walked back to the old Ford.

The previous fall the chief of this particular tribe wanted a boy child to take his place and one of his half dozen wives delivered a child to him. It was not a boy child so it could not take the chief's place and that angered the chief. He got drunk and put the baby girl child into a burlap bag took her out onto the ice and cut a hole and dropped her bag tied with rocks into the hole. The chief stayed drunk most of the time thereafter and after breakup in the late spring the women made a grappling hook and recovered the body from the bottom of the lake. When the infant body was recovered the chief went on another drunken binge and had not been seen for more than a week. The young man that had ushered us into the women's hut, also took us to the burial site and the spirit house where the infant was to be laid to rest. It was quite impressive and the spirit house looked a lot like a dog house. I shall never forget that experience either.

CHAPTER 8

Ice road trucking

The first winter I was in Red Lake I went to work for a big man named Earl Carvert. He was a gentle giant of a man about 6 feet, 7 inches tall and a devout Christian. He had been a hangman for the Canadian government and he never did tell me how many people he hung. He owned North American Lumber Company and he hired me to drive truck on weekends and summers when school was out. One Saturday morning he asked me to take the ice road (across Red Lake) and deliver a load of lumber and building supplies to the Madsen Gold Mine. You may know, that in the winter time the sun did not come up until late morning and at 7 AM, I was on my way across the frozen lake with my load and in darkness. I unloaded at the Madsen Mine and was heading back to Red Lake. I was about halfway across the lake when I noticed the ice in front of me was all red and when I stopped I realized it was blood. I got out of the truck and took a closer look around and discovered a pack of wolves had chased a deer across the lake but when his hooves hit the slick smooth ice road he fell and the wolves devoured him right there on the road. All that was left of the deer was a skeleton of bones and hair and blood. There was no sign of the wolves anywhere as they had already left the scene. I ventured off the ice road to follow the wolf trail and the best I could figure there were 7 wolves in the pack. It was almost 9:15 AM and the sun was coming up. It had to be about 7:30 AM when I crossed the lake going over to the Madsen Mine. Those wolves had attacked, killed and completely devoured that deer in less than two hours.

On another occasion I was crossing the ice road on a Saturday morning and this time I saw a pickup truck parked out in the middle of the lake. There was a couple sitting in the pickup and the motor was running and they waved at me as I drove by so I didn't stop. It was about 2 hours later I was returning to Red Lake and when I got to the middle of the lake the pickup was still sitting there and the engine was still running but I couldn't see anyone inside the truck so I stopped to take a closer look. I walked up to the driver's door and opened it. There was a white man lying on top of an Indian woman, both with their pants down, and both were very dead! As I learned later from the RCMP's, the exhaust had come up through the floor boards and had killed them both. It was a shocking experience for a 16 year old young man who lived a rather sheltered life in years prior.

CHAPTER 9

Chased by a Lynx!

When Uncle Victor heard we were moving to Red Lake he decided to give me some things he no longer needed. He had been in the Naval Air Force during WWII. Among some of the things he gave me were the following items. A WWII military issue K-Bar knife, a leather flight jacket with sheep's wool lining, a lemon wood long bow with a dozen arrows and a book on how to survive in the wilderness. I still have everything in my possession accept the flight jacket which has worn out many years ago. I loved that bow and arrow set. I spent many hours practicing with it and I did become very proficient with it. One winter day I went on a Raven hunt with my bow. I was determined to shoot a Raven!!! I started out by climbing the big rock behind our house and headed due north. I hadn't gone a half mile when I came upon a stand of cedars. There was a lot of snow on the ground and it was crusty but I was able to stay on top of the crust without breaking through. I noticed a lot of blood on the snow and there were big bones lying around and a lot of white and gray hair. It appeared to be Caribou hair. I nocked an arrow thinking I would see a Raven but there was not a sound to be heard. Then I noticed big chunks of snow falling down from the Cedar foliage above and it was falling closer and closer. I looked up in time to see some branches moving almost directly above my head. Then I made out a dark object and as I focused on it I suddenly saw what was sending the snow chunks to the ground! It was a Lynx!!!!! I did not have any broad heads on my arrows as they were all tipped with field (target) tips. I decided my best move would be to get out of his territory (dining room) as quickly as I could! I started to run and he was keeping up with me in the treetops for a short distance but then he stopped. I did not stop but continued to run all the way home and right into our kitchen. I must have scared mother because I told her I was just chased by a Lynx! I know she believed me because she said I was as white as a sheet.

That was the first and only Lynx I ever saw in the wild. I never went into the bush without broad head tips on my arrows again.

CHAPTER 10

Nantucket Sleigh Ride

I would guess this occurred in the summer of 56 or the early spring of 57. Chris Schantz and I were once again in Minnesota for a week or more of R&R. We knew an old man there who was a true logger and tree fell'er. A tree fell'er is one who fall's trees. In those days they were "fell" the hard way, with an axe and a wedge. Chris and I would stand directly under the tree as it began its fall. The old man had a very high voice and when we would do this his voice became even higher as he would yell at us hysterically to get out from under the tree. At our age we didn't realize the danger of what we were doing but thanks to God we never got hurt.

It was on one of these forays to Loman Minnesota that Chris and I were out on a lake fishing one day. We were in an old wooden row boat with a 7 1/2 or 10 HP engine. We weren't catching a lot of fish but we were always having fun and this day was no different. Suddenly we saw a moose swimming across the lake. It was about a mile across and Chris got the great idea to lasso the moose with the anchor rope and take advantage of a free ride to shore. Since I was an old horseman for my young years and familiar with lasso's I volunteered to do the roping. Chris brought the boat almost directly aside the swimming Moose and I was amazed at how wide his bloodshot eyes were as I lowered the loop over his head. Actually it might have been her head as there were no antlers and if it was early spring neither sex would have been bearing antlers. Well, needless to say the race was on. Chris shut the engine off and I was surprised how fast we were going! I had no idea that Moose could swim that fast! We were laughing and yelling "Gee" and "Haw" (a command given to sled dogs to turn left or right) but our commands fell on deaf ears as the Moose plowed straight ahead towards the shore which still seemed a good ways off.

By this time he was huffing and puffing pretty good and once in a while he made a guttural sound that sent chills up our spine. Then without warning and while we were still a good ways off from the shoreline the boat began to lurch forward in short spurts and then the huge shoulders of the giant Moose became bigger and bigger and we realized he was no longer swimming but now he was touching bottom and we were picking up speed. While Chris was fumbling to open his pen knife to cut the rope we hit shore (mostly rocks) and were on our way up the shallow bank and into the bush just feet behind the flailing legs of a now irritated and panicked Moose! I was sure the boat was ruined as I heard some really strange sounds as we bounced off huge rocks and trees before Chris finally sawed through the anchor rope and we were left sitting in a now motionless boat and the Moose disappeared into the thick bush never to be seen again.

It took Chris and I about an hour to get the boat back into the water and of course you know it was leaking like crazy!!! We had to empty the worm bucket over the side with all our worms in it and used it to bail the water out of the boat as we made our way back across the lake to where we had parked the car. The boat was not a complete loss but we never could get all the leaks fixed and we seldom used that boat again. Chris and I both agreed that we would never again lasso a moose for a free ride. Is it not amazing what a young person will do for enjoyment? Somehow something has changed over the years. Young people today seem more interested in taking drugs for excitement then seeking true adventure and exciting experiences to pass their time. I feel sorry for this new generation of young ones that have no idea of work ethics or what institutes high adventure. They have no idea what they are missing!

All things considered we were very lucky!

CHAPTER 11

My very first bear

I t was autumn, following our arrival in Red Lake that I had
the opportunity to go on my first serious bear hunt. I had
met an Indian man who called himself "Cowboy Pete"
soon after my introduction to Red Lake. Unlike most Ojibwa
Indians he was a strikingly good looking man. He had steel gray
eyes and though I was just 16 years of age and he being about
28 winters old (in his words) we formed a good friendship. He
spoke enough English as well as the Ojibwa language and that
we were able to communicate quite well. He had me speaking
broken Ojibwa in about 6 or 8 months. (something I have long
since mostly forgot). He took it upon himself to teach me the
basics of hunting and walking silently through the bush. He
was married to a very old white woman called Grace. I never
saw any affection between them but he was so proud to have a
white squall and she was proud to have a young good looking
husband. (Indian or not)!

When Cowboy Pete and I went hunting she always made
us manuck or cookies or something to eat while we were in
the bush.

One spring afternoon he stopped by our cabin to ask if I wanted to go bear hunting with him. I never had to be asked twice if I wanted to go hunting as it was one of my most favorite things to do. I grabbed my long bow and arrows and he quickly said "no, we are using guns today". We left our cabin and walked across town and out in the bush to his house. (shack)! We went inside and Grace was just finishing up baking the manuck.

Cowboy Pete picked up his trusty 22 caliber rifle and he gave me an old 30 caliber lever action rifle. After pocketing the banuck and saying good bye to Grace we were off. I must tell you about cowboy Pete's 22 caliber rifle. It was an old gun and the stock had been broken in half many years before. (probably in a fight or something). Anyway Cowboy Pete had removed the old stock and had taken a large branch from a tree with a crook in it (like a sling shot). He carved it to fit in the mounting on the hardware of the rifle and the crook was the part that fit on his arm at the shoulder. He shot moose, deer, caribou and bear with that 22 rifle hitting all the game in their ear for an instant kill. The gun looked stupid but it was extremely effective for him.

Anyway it was with some surprise that we went to the cyanide flats to hunt rather than into the bush. The cyanide flats were a result of the gold mining process many years before and it is basically a very fine sand that was pumped with water into the bush after it was ground up and all the gold removed. It is also the place the residents of Red Lake dumped all their garbage. On any given day you would see Indian women scouring through the garbage looking for eatable items discarded by white people, or they were looking for items that would make for a good substance for fermenting to make their own booze. Bear also found the area a good place to get a free meal and they were there on a very frequent basis.

We had arrived at about the middle of this 40 acre flat of cyanide when Pete motioned me to sit down. There are no trees growing in the cyanide flats as the cyanide killed all the trees years ago. So there we sat in the wide open fully visible to any bear that would venture onto the flats. We had a good view of the tree line that was a couple hundred yards away and it wasn't long when we saw a bear slowly coming out of the bush and into the tall grass that grew close to the tree line. Just on our side of the tall grass there was a stream that had cut its way through the cynide and the stream had cut the stream bed about six feet deep. There was a steep bank on our side but on the far side of the stream it was a gentle slope up to the tall grass. We watched the bear for a while as she lay down in the tall grass and soon we saw her feet in the air as she rolled around. Then we saw the reason for her ecstasy!!! With her, were three small cubs and they climbed onto her belly and began to nurse. Cowboy Pete quickly told me we would not be shooting that bear with cubs. We watched them for a long time and suddenly the sow jumped up and took off running back into the bush. I looked at Pete to get the answer for their quick departure but he was watching intently to the tree line. It was then, that the sow's quick departure became evident. Out of the bush came a huge boar bear as he waddled into the tall grass. He stopped and smelled the area the sow had been laying but he seemed more interested in eating garbage then finding a mother bear. He slowly walked his way down the slope and into the stream bed and out of sight, hidden by the steep bank on our side of the stream. I scampered to my feet and was about to run over to the bank and shoot down at the bear when Pete grabbed my jacket and yanked me off my feet. The look he gave me with those steel gray eyes said it all and he did not have to say a word. I had just been chastised by him and he never said a word. It was a lesson I never forgot!!!

Patience is required when hunting bear!!! We sat there in silence for what seemed like hours but it was more like a few minutes when the huge shoulders of that bear came into view over the bank. There he was standing and looking right at us. My heart was pounding out of my chest and when I looked over at Pete he was as calm as a cucumber. I wanted to shoot but he whispered "NO" and soon the bear tired of looking over the cyanide flats and started moving in our direction. He continued to glance in our direction as he came towards us but Pete demanded I stay still.

Finally I could take it no longer and I jumped to my feet and began shooting. As soon as my feet were under me the big boar was in a full run back towards the stream bed. I was shooting as fast as I could pump another round into the chamber. The bear rolled a couple of times but continued towards the bank and out of sight down into the stream bed. I was running after him, shooting and I emptied all the bullets in my gun. I was reloading my rifle as I was running and managed to get about three more bullets into it. I fired off three more shots and the bear finally went down kicking. Suddenly Pete was standing next to me and with one shot from his 22 the bear lay dead!!! Pete looked at me with a look I hope I never see again as long as I live. It was filled with disdain and anger!!! He never said a word and he didn't have to. His eyes said it all. Later he told me he had decided then, that he would never hunt with me again but thank goodness he changed his mind. After we skinned the bear we found seven bullet holes in him with only three holes being potential killing shots which included the one bullet fired by Pete's 22 right in the ear. I think I fired nine shots all together. Three of them missed him completely and four of them hit his legs and rump. One went through his guts and one went through his liver. The 22 caliber from Pete's gun went into the brain.

This began my love for bear hunting! It provides an adrenalin rush that few other animals come close to creating and I suppose the reason for that is the fact the bear can actually kill you and eat you! Not a good outcome but there within lays the excitement of hunting bear not for the faint of heart.

CHAPTER 12

Leaving home

I left home and the Village of Red Lake in 1957 and made my way to Goshen Indiana. I was 17 years old at the time. My mother's brother, (my uncle John C. Wenger) resided there and he was a professor at Goshen College. I had spent a year studying under the British educational system which is far advanced from the American system I had been accustomed to for the first 9 years of my education.

For example I went into the 11th grade when I arrived in Red Lake and my classes consisted of 4th year Latin, 6th year French, 3rd year Algebra, English prose and poetry, British history and Advanced Science. I managed to graduate but I don't know how because I did not pass French or Latin, although I had one year of Latin at Pennridge High School before moving to Red Lake. It was just too big a jump to go from one year to fourth year in one step. When I arrived in Goshen I enrolled at a private school by the name of Bethany Christian High School and after testing was moved to the 12th grade. Uncle John arranged for me to live at one of his friend's house which had an apartment in the basement. It was quite

36

comfortable for me especially after living in the primitive cabin at Red Lake with no hot running water or an indoor bathroom. I believe if I recall correctly I paid $12.00 a week for rent while living there. I was given no money when I left home so I had no money and needed a job to survive. My school also required tuition and although it was very inexpensive I needed a job in order to pay for that as well. Jobs for 17 year old kids were not that easy to come by and I wound up getting a job starting at 6 PM and ending at 1 AM the following morning. It was a job, setting up pins at a bowling alley and I was in charge of 4 alleys at one time. It kept you running and if I made $45.00 a week that seems about right. I worked 6 days a week. The problems really started when I was found falling asleep in the classroom. I was called into the principal's office to explain myself. When I mentioned that I needed to work to pay my rent and tuition the principle reminded me that there was a curfew for students living off campus and I had to be in bed by 10: PM. I think he was going to make an exception to that rule when he noticed I was wearing a ring on my right hand ring finger. He raised his voice and said "is that a ring I see on your finger! I raised my right hand and took a long look at my ring and said "yes sir, that's what it appears to be" in a rather sarcastic voice. This angered him I guess and he proceeded to tell me I could not attend his school wearing a ring. I reluctantly removed the ring from my finger and put it in my pocket. I was dismissed from his office and went back to class fully awake by this time. By now my anger was building up and revenge was in my mind. I had met several other kids my age at the bowling alley and one of these young fellows had a 1953 ford with a thunderbird engine. It was "souped up" as they called it in those days. It was a pale green and white car with lots of chrome. The kid that owned that car and the friends he hung around with are what my dear late mother would call the "bad crowd". I however was kind of proud to be associated with such a renowned group of young men.

I decided I was working too hard and needed a break so I decided to only work from Monday through Friday from now on. That would kill two birds with one stone. It would show the principle that I could do what I wanted and he could do nothing about it. It also gave me weekends off to hang around with my new found friends the "bad crowd". We sure had fun!!! On Saturday nights we decided it would be fun to steal watermelons and tomatoes from the many farmers in the surrounding area. It is easy to say that "boys will be boys" but I am here to tell you there is truth in that statement. There were four of us and we would drive about 20 miles from Goshen and the driver would leave three of us off on a particular road near a watermelon field or tomato field. We would fill our bags with ripe tomatoes and when we were ready to be picked up we would lay a stick on the road where the driver dropped us off and we would wait for him to return and pick us up. We would pile back in the car with our bags of tomatoes or arms full of watermelons. Then we would drive down the road in the darkness and when a car was approaching us we would lob a few tomatoes at the oncoming windshield and we could hear the splat as the tomatoes splattered across the oncoming car. Our driver would floor the accelerator and away we went, down unknown roads in the dark at breakneck speed. Why we never wrecked I will never know because there was no reason we shouldn't have.

Sometimes we would go to the railroad tracks and wait for a train and as the train was passing we would wait until we saw a car with a passenger sleeping with his head against the window. Of course he was then the target and he would waken quickly from the sound and see nothing but tomato juice and seeds sliding down his window. We thought it was great fun!!!

I still wanted my revenge however for the principle of Bethany Christian High School. I was again wearing my ring but he had not yet caught me.

By this time a month had gone by and we were becoming famous. There were articles in the local papers around Goshen about a gang of thieves, stealing watermelons and tomatoes. I felt like Jesse James must have felt. Then on Saturday night I came up with a brilliant idea. Let's steal about six watermelons and take them to Bethany Christian High School. When we arrived at the school we drove with our lights out through the parking lot and when we came close to the double doors at the front entrance we got out with our six watermelons. There was a crack at the bottom of the doors with about a quarter inch of space between the door and the threshold. Together we smashed the watermelons against the concrete and door and the seeds and juices went skidding up the highly polished tile floors inside the school building. We were really having fun now, especially me and we kept throwing watermelons until they were all gone. What a mess we made.

Our frustrations released we decided we made enough havoc that night and we began our ride back to the town of Goshen. We were driving slowly so as not to attract attention when we heard a siren. From behind us came an ambulance or a police car with his siren wailing! I, for one got chills that I still feel today when I think back on that experience. The first vehicle went past us at very high speed and it was a police car. The second vehicle was an ambulance. Both with red lights flashing and sirens blowing!!! All four of us were sobered up from all the fun and laughter almost instantly!!! About a mile further we saw the police car and the ambulance parked in front of a church. Their lights were still flashing and there was a crowd of people standing there. We drove up slowly and decided to park on a side street. We still had the floor in the back seat area of the car, full of tomatoes. We parked the car and made our way to where the crowd was gathered. As we got closer we could see a young man lying in front of the church register which was lit up and he appeared to be hurt real bad. As we got closer we saw his belly was all bloody. They had cut some of his pants and shirt away so they could administer first aid. We could hear the policeman interviewing a middle aged man and we drew closer to hear what was being said.

It turned out the man heard a noise outside his back door and when he turned on the outside lights he saw two young men stealing his car. He reached behind the door and grabbed his shotgun and fired at rather close range. The shot hit the oldest boy just above his left hip and the pellets cut his wide belt in half and blew some of his belly area completely away! His younger brother it turned out picked him up from the ground and over his shoulders he carried him until he finally dropped him in front of the church register. Soon the ambulance departed with the boy and the cop that was doing the interview took the middle aged man in his car and left. By this time there were cops all over the place and we decided we better be moving on. Were we ever in for a surprise when we got back to the car to find we had a flat tire. Here we were four young lads with muddy shoes and a car with the floor in the back seat area full of tomatoes and we have a flat tire with cops walking all around! To make matters even worse this souped up car had flipper hub caps and to keep the hub caps from being stolen the owner had valve stem locks on all four wheels. The real problem was he did not bring the key so there was no way to get the hubcap off. In desperation he reached into his pocket and came out with a knife! With it he cut the valve stem off the tire and we were able to change the tire and get out of there before we got caught. It was a lesson I will never forget and I dropped my new found friends the next day.

When I arrived at school on Monday morning the janitor was cleaning up the watermelon mess we had made and I had to fight to keep from smiling. The experience of the night before still had me on edge and I decided I needed new friends so I ended my criminal behavior.

Several weeks later the principle again called me to his office. Someone, probably a teacher, had told him I was again wearing the ring and he demanded I take it off. I told him I was not going to do that and he said then you will be expelled. I said "fine" and proceeded to clean out my desk. I took all my books that I had bought home and then went to the bowling alley and resigned. I returned to my basement apartment and packed all my things and said good bye to my wonderful landlords, Mr. and Mrs. Swartzendruber.

With my bags in hand I walked to the turnpike several miles away and hitched a ride on a hog truck to Pennsylvania. I did a lot of hitch hiking in those days.

CHAPTER 13

Back in Pennsylvania

I must have only stood at the on ramp of the Indiana turnpike for less than 30 minutes when I saw a big hog truck heading east. I stuck out my thumb and I saw the driver hit the brakes and wave at me as he roared past coming to a stop a few hundred feet past me. I was already running as fast as I could with my suit case in hand. I climbed up on this big truck and the driver said 'where are you heading young man' and I told him Pennsylvania. He too, was going to Pennsylvania so I loaded my suit case into the sleeper and took my seat on the passenger side of the cab. I was amazed at how many times he had to shift gears before we got to 55 MPH. I remember wondering how he could know where all those gears were to be found. We talked for hours and soon I was sound asleep. When I awoke I was surprised we were already in western Pennsylvania. It was dark outside and one look at my watch told me it was just past three o'clock in the morning. The driver was glad I was awake and we again talked. I told him of my life in Red Lake and my experience at Bethany Christian High school. He told me that he makes this trip twice weekly and he uses "Bennies" to stay awake for the long drive from Chicago to Pennsylvania. This load of hogs we had on this trip, were going to Philadelphia. I asked if he was going to be using route 309 south from where the turn pike crosses that road and he said he was. I told him he could leave me off at that junction and he agreed. It was so easy to hitch hike in those days when we were safe from dangerous people, unlike today. When I was dropped off at route 309 I hitched a ride to Souderton, PA and walked to a former neighbor's house on 113 where I stayed for a few weeks.

He gave me a car to drive while I was there and I drove to Pennridge High School where I spoke with the principle, a Mr. Rosenkrantz. Without hesitation he made it clear that he would not allow me to go to school there as long as my parents were still living in Canada. I explained to him over and over that my father still owns the house on route 113 and was paying taxes on that property which included school taxes. It didn't make any difference to Rosenkrantz he was not about to let me in. So, it was then I decided I must go to work. I had a puppy love crush on a girl named Bette when I was in the 10th grade and I remembered that she lived in Bedminster, near Dublin. I had some extra money left over from my job in Indiana and I bought a Cushman scooter from a scooter store for$25.00. Gasoline was around .20 cents a gallon and a gallon of gas took me and that scooter about 65 miles. I went to see Bette. She seemed happy to see me again and we began dating almost immediately. She was very understanding when I told her I could not go back to school because of Rosenkrantz and that I needed a job and a place to live. To my surprise she said that I could live at her brother's house which was just a mile away from where she lived with her parents and younger brothers. Her brother's name was Emerson and his wife's name was Dorothy. They had an extra bedroom so they rented me the room and board for $25.00 a month if I recall. I wanted to drive truck but at 17 years of age I was not old enough. Finally I landed a job as a laborer at the local grocery store in Dublin. I was stocking shelves and doing any other odd jobs they wanted me to do and although it was not my dream job it did offer me a steady income. My little Cushman scooter did a fine job of getting me from point A to point B but it sure did not keep me dry on rainy days. I was now a working man with a steady income and I decided I needed a car. I had asked Dorothy if she could give me two pint mason jars with lids and she did. In my closet in my bedroom there was a shelf above the cloths rod and I nailed the mason jar lids to the bottom side of the the shelf. Every Friday, which was payday I would take the appropriate amount of cash and put it in the mason jar labeled "Rent". I then would put living expense money into the second jar named "Savings". Over the months that followed I accumulated just under $1000.00 in my Savings jar and I went car shopping. I found a 1955 Oldsmobile 88 convertible that was pretty and it was red and white with a red and white leather interior and a white top. I loved that car and wished I still owned it. I sold my scooter for$50.00 since I had it repainted and new tires put on it and now I had a car. Bette and I were getting closer and closer. I was spending more and more time at her house and especially when her parents were not home.

This arrangement worked out well for us but not too well in the long run. There is an old saying that goes something like this when it comes to child birth. "The first one can come anytime but all the rest take nine months"! Well, such was the case for Bette and I and I was a bit stunned when she told me she was pregnant. I was just 18 years old and Bette was 17. Way too young to start a family but being raised and taught to be a responsible person I did what was expected of me and Bette and I were married in June of 1958. True to the old saying our firstborn was a daughter we named Sandra Lee. She was as cute as a pin but she suffered a lot from colic and cried a lot.

A year later God blessed us with another daughter and we named her Sherry Denise. She too was as cute as a pin but she and Sandy were as different as night and day. Sandy was the motherly type from the very beginning and although she had just learned to walk herself she wanted to carry Sherry or hold her on her lap.

True to form, a year and four months later God blessed us with yet another child and this one was a boy. We named him Steven Merrill. I was a proud father and especially glad to have a son that could carry my name but not necessarily my weaknesses.

As the years drifted by each of the children were developing their own personalities. Sherry was the very smart one with a witty answer to almost every question. Sandy, or "Sam" as she liked to be called, remained the motherly type and continued to look after her two younger siblings. Steve was all boy and wanted to play ball, ride the horse and do all that he saw his father do.

By now I was employed by Brooks Instruments Company in Hatfield, PA. I was an instrument engineer, having achieved my high school diploma through the GED program. I enjoyed that job immensely and the owner of the company, Mr. Douglas Brooks took notice of me and apparently liked what he saw. I had framed photos of horses on my desk and he noticed them and invited me to visit his farm in upstate NY where he kept thoroughbred brood mares.

By this time in our lives, Bette and I were not getting along too well. We realized too late that our marriage at the age of 17 and 18 was too young to make life changing decisions. Mr. Brooks also noticed that I was going through a difficult time at home and he asked me if I would be interested in opening a sales office for Brooks Instruments in Houston, Texas. I jumped at the opportunity and it was arranged that in March of 1968 I would be moved to Houston. I had an apartment in Lansdale, PA, a short distance from Hatfield and one day Mayflower Moving and Storage arrived and loaded all my furniture for the trip to Houston. I was given Brooks Instrument credit cards and after a tearful goodbye to my children, off I went in my 1966 Thunderbird headed for Houston Texas.

For years prior to having a direct office in Houston, we were represented there by a company called Gaye Engineering and Sales, a manufacturer's representative. I had been in telephone contact many times, over the years with that company and always dealt with a nice lady named Ann Woods. Ms. Woods was kind enough to mail me the want ads of the Houston Post newspaper and from that paper I found an apartment complex that I felt I would like living at and calling it my home.

After arriving in Houston I checked into the Marriott Hotel, which would be my home for the next month and set out to find an appropriate location for a sales office. After a lot of searching and comparing I finally settled on a location on Yoakum Blvd and negotiated a lease agreement. I spent the next couple weeks finding office furniture and equipment and stocking shelves with the required office supplies. Then I hired a secretary and the following Monday we opened the doors of Brooks Instruments in Houston, Texas.

Then I went to 9900 on Memorial Drive and was stunned by the beauty of this huge complex which took the entire country block. The address was on the outskirts of Houston in a more rural setting with lots of trees and gardens. It was a brand new facility and as yet there were no occupants. There were over 1000 apartments in this complex and it was designed for single people or newlyweds with no children. I chose a second floor apartment with my front door porch overlooking a beautiful garden and my back door offering a balcony overlooking a beautiful swimming pool. A phone call later and my furniture were scheduled to be delivered the following day. I was finally all settled in at my new and exciting location, Houston, Texas.

Little did I realize then how very hot the weather gets there in the summer or how many things that walk and crawl are poisonous!!!

CHAPTER 14

The losers club

It was a cold winter day for Houston with the temperature in the low 60's. Bob came over with his "Manhattan" firmly in his grip. Bob Lohman was one of the first people to move into the brand new apartments at 9900 on Memorial Drive after I moved in. He was a corporate attorney for very large petro chemical company. Literally every time I saw him he was holding a glass with a perfectly mixed Manhattan in his hand. Super Bowl Sunday was coming up and Bob wanted someone to accompany him to Dallas to enjoy the game at his friend's house. We were going to be staying at the Ramada Inn on Stemens freeway. At least I was because he had a new girlfriend who resided in Dallas and the chances were that he would be staying with her. Not learning until after we arrived in Dallas Friday afternoon that Bob had made plans for Saturday night. That plan was for a double date with me and a blind date that Bob's girlfriend had arranged. How could she do this as she had never met me!!! Anyway being the mild mannered person that I am I accepted the fate that was laid out for me without an argument.

The date was to be a dinner occasion with drinks at a club afterwards.

Saturday evening came and Bob and his girlfriend picked me up at the Ramada Inn and we drove across town to pick up my blind date. We arrived and I went dutifully to the door and was met by this short, fat and not really that attractive girl. I introduced myself and she replied her name was Beverly but preferred Bev for short! I knew immediately this was a big mistake and I was going to kill my friend Bob later! If he did this to be funny I would get even I assure you!

We had an uneventful dinner with Bob and his girlfriend doing most of the talking. The evening was dragging on and on. Every time I looked at my watch at what I thought to be an hour later, the minute hand had only moved ten minutes. Finally dinner was over and we drove to a night club for drinks. I was almost going to say that my dinner was making me ill so I could end this punishment but decided to stick it out. We drove into this huge parking lot that was fairly full of cars and I could not help but notice the big neon sign that spelled out "THE LOSER'S CLUB"! I absolutely could not believe my eyes! How absolutely appropriate was this! We walked in and checked the ladies jackets and were escorted to a table. All the tables in the joint were built like picnic tables. There was a band on stage that was warming up their instruments. This was definitely going to be a very long evening!!! Soon a cute waitress brought our drinks and I was enjoying the delightful way she smiled and moved which got my mind off the reality of my situation! Soon the band started playing and Bob and his date stood up and went dancing. I told Bev that I couldn't dance and that gave me a good excuse to stay seated. I ordered another round! By the third dance I was on my fourth drink and was now having doubles! All that booze was not helping at all. I found myself staring at Bev to see if I could find anything attractive about her but that was an exercise in futility. I was beginning to get that "glow" one gets when the alcohol really starts hitting your blood vessels and girls all begin to look good no matter how ugly they may be. I wanted to be anywhere but here! I took a deep sigh and looked straight ahead and there facing me were two of the most beautiful blonde girls I have seen in a long time. This definitely was not the booze this was for real! Interestingly they were both looking at me! I smiled and they smiled back, especially the one on the left! I looked around for a sign of a bathroom and found it all the way across the dance floor. I excused myself from Bev and made my way towards the sign. To get to the bath rooms you had to climb three steps and the men's room was down a short hallway to the left the women's room to the right. When I reached the top of the third step I turned around and looked back at the blonde girls and the blonde on the left was still looking at me. I tilted my head back a bit and smiled and I saw her get up and start towards me. I ducked behind the wall at the top of the steps and waited. I didn't wait long and here came the beauty I was smiling to. She stepped around the corner where I was standing and said "who is that you are with, your mother"? I said "no, that is my first blind date and it will be my last"! She asked where I was from and I said Houston. She then asked where I was staying and I told her the Ramada Inn on the Stemens Freeway. Then she really surprised me by saying "what are you doing later"? Later! It was already 11:45 PM! I told her 'nothing', that I was going back to my hotel. She wrote down my name and room number and said "see you later" with the cutest smile I ever saw! She spun around and disappeared into the ladies room. I stepped into the men's room and since I really did not have to go I washed my hands and walked back to my table. I was suddenly stone sober. Bob was back from the dance floor and the two girls got up from our table and went to the ladies room. I told Bob I wanted to go that I was not having a good time. I couldn't tell him the real reason for surely he would screw it up somehow.

He laughed and said he understood and when the ladies returned we got their jackets and left. Since we were going by the Ramada Inn before we got to Bev's house I was dropped off and I thanked Bev for a wonderful evening and went to my room.

I knew I would never hear from Janet again (the gorgeous blonde from the Losers Club) so I got undressed and was climbing into bed when my phone rang. I answered it and it was the front desk. I was told there was someone in the lobby that wanted to see me. I said I would be down in a few minutes and excitedly climbed back into my clothes and headed for the front desk expecting to see Janet in all her beauty standing there. Instead there stood a man in a black suit wearing a chauffeur's hat. When I was approaching the front desk he said "are you Mr. Rosenberger"? I said that indeed I was and he said that Janet had sent him here to pick me up! Holy smoke! I couldn't believe it! We walked out the main entrance and there was a big black stretched limousine and he opened the back door and I got in. I was all alone! Janet was not in the car! We drove for almost 30 minutes and were entering a very exclusive neighborhood! The mansions that lined both sides of the road were all lit up with lights shining on them to show them off! I was impressed! We drove into a long looping driveway with a covered runway over the drive at the main entrance of the mansion and the driver stopped the limo, got out and opened my door. He walked with me to the door and before he could open the door, it opened! There stood Janet and she was wearing a see through floor length night gown and very little more! I entered the foyer and one look to my left revealed a huge Grand Piano! Straight ahead was a long spiral staircase which Janet was leading me to. As we were walking she said "I sent James to pick you up, I hope you don't mind". Of course not, I replied. She went on to explain that this was her parents' house and they were out of the country for the month and she was 'house sitting' for them! Needless to say I spent an enjoyable night at Janet's house and nearly missed the "Super Bowl" the following day. When I arrived back at the Ramada the following afternoon Bob was almost about to call the police and report me missing!

I started dating Janet for a short time but broke it off after watching her drinking habits. Our relationship would never work with the amount of booze she consumed on a regular basis. It all started at the "Loser's Club" anyway! I swore no more blind dates!

CHAPTER 15

Meeting Donna

Sometime after I moved into 9900 On Memorial Drive I noticed what appeared to be a couple moving in, to a second floor apartment, adjacent to mine. The girl was on the short side but she looked really cute!

I never had much of a single life because it wasn't too long after I left home and went through the experiences in Indiana that I found myself married to Bette. As a result I had to take responsibility for my own domestic chores. Like clockwork I did my wash on a Friday afternoon and always did my ironing on Saturday morning. I washed dishes after every meal and I vacuumed the carpet and dusted on Friday afternoons while doing my laundry. The apartment complex had many laundry mats scattered throughout and the nearest one was very close to the apartment of the couple that had just moved in. So I came home from work on a Friday afternoon went into my apartment and undressed completely. I jumped into my sweat pants and made a bee line for the laundry mat to wash every piece of washable clothes and underwear that I had worn that week.

About three weeks later I had no sooner arrived at the laundry room that Friday, with my load of wash, dressed only in my sweat pants and here came the cute little girl that I watched moving in a few weeks prior. She had a huge smile and said "hi" in a very Texas accent. I returned the greeting and she said again "Hi my name is Drue" as she stuck her hand out and I shook her hand and told her mine. She definitely was a Cutie! I was looking for her left hand to see if she was wearing a ring but she had both hands behind her butt as she was leaning against a washer. She asked what I did for a living and I told her. She explained that she was an assistant manager of the flight attendants for Continental Airlines based at the Houston International Airport.

All the while we were talking she kept her hands hidden behind her back and I was getting more and more curious. Finally I couldn't wait any longer so I asked "what does your husband do"? I must say it was with some disappointment when she replied that he was a professional student at Rice University. Well, that settled that subject and for some reason I noticed she was no longer hiding her hands. Of course that may have been my wild imagination! In any case we hit it off pretty good and we became very good friends. Drinks in my apartment became a fairly regular occurrence at least several times a week from then on and although I had not yet met her husband I did learn that his name was Pete.

One Saturday afternoon she came over for a drink and she asked me about a couple girls she had seen coming into my apartment from time to time. I told her they were just friends (and they were) and Drue said, "you could do better Merrill". That threw me for a loop because any girl I dated was attractive and the girls that were visiting me were all very good looking. She than asked me if I had ever had a blind date. I told her that I had experienced one and that it was a disaster. (Although it ended very well, but that was a previous chapter). I did not go into detail about my first blind date. Anyway she asked me if I would be interested in meeting her secretary, Donna. She went on and on about how beautiful she was and how nice a person she was.

I liked Drue and respected her and out of that respect I agreed to meet her secretary. She went on to say how mature for her age she was, which prompted me to ask her age and Drue replied that she was 21 years old. (I was 30 at the time). Drue insisted our age difference would not present a problem for Donna if it did not for me, so the plans proceeded.

In any case several weeks later, on one of Drue's visits she asked me if the following Saturday night would suit me to come to her and Pete's for cocktails and dinner. She had also invited Bob Loman and his lady friend Lil. I agreed and the date was set.

Well, Saturday night came and I went over to Drue and Pete's at the invited time. Bob and Lil were already there and I finally got to meet Pete, the elusive student. Sitting on the Davenport was a very good looking young lady that I knew had to be my date and I was impressed! Drue took my hand and led me over and introduced me to Donna Rae Elenga. I said hello as I took her hand in both of mine and sat down beside her. We spent the entire evening talking to each other and enjoyed an Italian dinner that Drue had worked hard all day to prepare. The evening came to a close way too soon and I could not believe how the time slipped away as it was midnight and Donna had a long drive home. I could not drive her as she had driven there in her own car but I did walk her to her car and thanked her for a wonderful evening. After wishing her a safe drive home I watched as she drove away in darkness.

Thus began my relationship with Donna Rae Elenga that resulted in our marriage almost a year later.

CHAPTER 16

My marriage to Donna

Donna and I dated for nearly a year before I finally fell to one knee and asked for her hand in marriage. She seemed happy at my gesture and said "yes" and I was overjoyed. We set the date of the wedding on September 11th, 1970. This was my second marriage. It was Donna's first marriage. I was 30 years of age and Donna was 21. She was the joy of my life and we loved each other with all our hearts. We both lived in Houston, Texas but I lived on the west side at the 9900 block of Memorial Drive and she still lived at home with her mother and step father on the other side of Houston. It was a long commute between our places of residence but we managed to see each other 4 to 5 days a week. My first wife was a wonderful woman as well but we both agreed that we married too young and were both confused by "puppy love" as to the real thing. We did have three beautiful children together and we remain distant friends to this day.

Donna, never having been married, wanted a big wedding and she certainly was entitled to one. She was born into a catholic family and was raised in that religion.

She wanted a catholic wedding and she was going to have one. We both went to her parish and spoke honestly about our desire to wed with the senior priest. After I told him I was divorced he refused to marry us in his church.

Donna would not take "no" for an answer and decided she would ask one of the younger priests at the same parish. She was able to arrange a meeting with Father Thomas for the both of us and we went to meet this young priest on a weekday evening. We must have spoken with him for more than an hour when he finally said that as much as we seemed to love each other there was nothing stopping us from getting married somewhere else so it should be at the Catholic Church and he would marry us. It would not be a high mass wedding though and we both agreed that was fine. The wedding plans continued and my parents agreed to fly from Pennsylvania to Texas for the wedding.

I asked one of my best friends (Bruce Spurlin) a colleague at Brooks Instruments in Pennsylvania if he would be willing to stand as my best man and he agreed.

Donna and I decided not to live in my one bedroom apartment on memorial drive but to find a two bedroom apartment closer to down town Houston which was closer to her employment locale, as was mine as well. I loved our new apartment but we did not share it prior to our wedding day. It had a gas or wood burning fireplace as well as a wet bar. In those days I enjoyed a cocktail before dinner and sometimes a night cap before bedtime. The wet bar was a treat!

Several days before the "big" day my parents arrived at Houston Intercontinental Airport and I was there to greet them. They stayed with me in our new apartment in the guest bedroom until our wedding day.

Our plans included a two week honeymoon at St. Thomas, Virgin Islands. We made reservations at Blue Beards Castle Hotel and chose the bridal suite as our residence while there.

Bruce arrived the day before the wedding and we were both fitted for our tuxedos.

That night we had our rehearsal followed by a wonderful rehearsal dinner. All were present including the brides maids, groomsmen and parents from both sides. Donna's mother was busy with the arrangements for the reception following the wedding and there was very little sleep for me or Donna that night with the excitement that was promised the following day. We had chosen our music including the September Song as the wedding song for Donna's and my first dance.

Finally the big day arrived and I had the jitters but no cold feet. True to tradition I did not see the bride since the night before and would not see her again until she began her walk down the isle with Herbert, her step father at the wedding.

Oh my God, was she beautiful!!!! I had not seen her look more beautiful and she took my breath away. It was a huge church and it was nearly filled to capacity.

Finally those words we both wanted so bad to hear, "I now pronounce you man and wife" and "you may kiss the bride". My mother was crying! So was Donna's mother!

The reception went off without a hitch! We not only had a wedding cake, Donna's mother had ordered a German chocolate cake for a groom's cake as well. The beverages served were champagne and soft drinks for those that did not use alcohol. Coffee was also available for those that wanted. There was more than ample amounts of ham, barbecued beef, potato salad and coleslaw for everyone. Afterwards, Donna and I left for our night stay at the Houston Marriott Hotel prior to our flight the next morning to St. Thomas, in the Virgin Islands.

Our honeymoon was almost like a dream. We had taken the bridal suite at the very top of the castle and we could stand on our balcony and see the cruise ships come and go. The water was so very blue. We drank exotic blue drinks that went down so smooth but kicked like a mule a bit later. We spent many hours on a deserted beach under the shade of the palm trees. We did a lot of snorkeling in the crystal clear and blue waters of the Caribbean. We took a tram ride up to the top of a mountain nearby and took photos from there and our way up.

The 14 day honeymoon seemed to be over almost as soon as it began and we had to make a stop at the liquor store for some duty free booze before boarding our flight back home to Texas.

It was important for me to be back in Houston by Monday morning because I needed to catch a flight to Atlanta, Georgia for a business convention, leaving my bride for a week of solitude without her.

We arrived back in Houston on Sunday afternoon and our lives as husband and wife began.

CHAPTER 17

Move to the pacific NW

It was Christmas time in 1970 and by this time Sally and Terry Rose had become very good friends of ours. Sally was Donna's boss and Terry was a few years older than me. Terry and I had a lot in common. We both had a love of the great outdoors and we both were expert at canoeing. He was a school teacher. As it turned out he and Sally were not originally from Texas and neither were Donna and I. We all disliked the humidity of Houston and I especially disliked the idea that everything that walked and crawled was poisonous. Soon after our marriage, Donna was gracious enough to accept my then eight year old son Steve into our family. When I think about that it almost brings tears to my eyes that a bride of just a few months would take on the responsibility of helping to raise a young boy who was struggling in school. He was failing in school and the principle of his school (Brooke Moyer) who was a friend of mine suggested that I take Steve to live with my new bride and me in Texas. He believed that the influence of his father would help him as he had two older sisters and a mother that all seemed to dominate him. Donna agreed to the addition and we flew Steve to Texas.

We enrolled him into the nearest school and set him up with a school bus ride every morning to school. Donna was his Tudor and with her help his grades took off in an upward spiral almost immediately. He liked Donna and Donna loved him too.

On Christmas eve we had Sally and Terry as our dinner guests and after dinner we were sitting around talking about the fact that none of us were from Texas and more than that neither of us were happy living there. When Brooks Instruments had first moved me there I replaced a manufactures representative that had represented Brooks for years. The income they produced for Brooks throughout the years of their efforts had never exceeded $300,000.00 per year. The first year of Brooks being directly represented with our own office the revenue rose to 1.2 million and was growing even higher the following year. For that reason I substantiated in my mind that I had no reason to feel guilty by resigning my position at Brooks and seeking employment in a new location. My efforts in Houston had long since paid for the cost to Brooks of moving me there. The four of us agreed that in 1971 our goal was to relocate to a place with a far better climate and less poisonous critters.

Our guests left for home at around 11:00 PM and Donna and I lay in bed talking about our future plans for a few more hours. The following morning after all the presents were opened Steve asked if he could ride his new bike to his friend's house and show him his new Christmas present. We agreed and away he went.

Donna and I continued our conversation about a new location for residence. She was born and raised in southern California and had no desire to return there. I certainly had no desire to return to Pennsylvania. Donna asked if I had ever been to Portland, Oregon and I replied that I had not. She suggested I fly to Portland the weekend after New Year's Day.

So the first weekend after the New Year, I boarded a plane and flew to Portland Oregon. Little did I know when I left Houston I was in for a big surprise awaiting me in Portland.

The flight to Portland had a short stop in Denver before going on. The captain made no announcement as we approached the Portland International Airport but when looking out the window as we were on our final approach I could see we were landing in a severe snow storm. We arrived at the terminal and began deplaning. I was in first class so I deplaned almost as the first one. I went to the Hotel phones and began calling for vacancies. One by one I was getting the same answer from them all. "Sorry no vacancy as there is a convention in town". Then I went to the phone book and after about 20 more calls with the same results I was doomed to sit the night out at the airport lobby. The following morning I boarded the first plane heading back to Houston going through Denver once again. Donna could clearly see that I was depressed when I arrived home. I told her I hated Portland and did not want to go back there. She was so gracious and told me not to worry, that next week I should try to go to Seattle. I agreed and the following Saturday morning I headed for the airport once again for a flight to Seattle. This time the results were entirely different. As the plane was circling Seattle for our final approach I was glued to the window and was thrilled at what I saw. It was a beautiful clear day and we were passing over lakes and snow covered mountain tops and I could see Mount Rainier in the distance that towered 14,500 feet high. I saw all the evergreen trees and the wilderness and knew this is where I wanted to live. The only thing that could stop me was not being able to find a job.

Our plane landed and we deplaned. I took a hotel limousine across the street to the Jet Inn and checked in for the weekend.

I purchased the three local newspapers, the Seattle Times, the Post Intelligencer and the Auburn/Kent newspaper. I went to my room and began scouring the classified ads for places of employment. My field of expertise was in instrumentation. There were six openings found for instrumentation and a position for a sales representative at Philippine Airlines. I sent seven resume's out to the hotel mail box and took a taxi ride around Seattle to get the lay of the land. I had my Texas address on each one of the resumes with an explanation that I was in the process of moving to Seattle. The following morning I took the limo back to Seatac Airport across the street and flew back to Houston, this time with a smile on my face.

Monday morning found me back at my desk at Brooks Instruments. I was in a terrific mood and even my secretary noticed it. I was determined that I was going to Seattle, job offer or not. Wednesday I received my first letter of response from one of the six instrument related companies. It was a firm offer but the money was nowhere close to what I was used to making. Thursday's mail brought 4 more responses to my resumes. Four more firm offers with only one of the offers showing any sign of life concerning the money I needed to earn. I was intrigued by the thought of employment at an airlines. I was praying I would get a letter response from them. Friday came and went and so did Saturday. Nothing more! By Wednesday of the following week I was sure I would not hear from the other two resume applications so I sent a letter of acceptance to the one instrument company that offered the best money. The John Marvin Company. I was thrilled and Donna too was happy at my fortunate employment opportunity.

I tendered my resignation to Brooks Instruments and began planning my move to Seattle. The John Marvin Co. was thrilled to have me come aboard because they represented among other things a company called Shute and Corting, a direct competitor to Brooks Instruments. The John Marvin Co was a manufacturer's representative.

It was decided that I would move to Seattle ahead of Donna and Steve and find a place to live and set up housekeeping. We would switch from week to week with me flying one weekend to Texas and the following weekend Donna and Steve would fly to Seattle.

I found a perfect two bedroom apartment in Bellevue, Washington and went to the furniture store and bought a dining room, living room and bedroom sets which were delivered a few days later and I could move from my hotel room to our new home in the Pacific N.W. Our plan was for Donna to transfer from Houston to Seattle, retaining her employment with Continental Airlines. Ideally she would stay in Houston with Steve until school was out for the summer so that we did not have to disrupt Steve's school year with yet another school change. I had left my 1966 Ford Thunderbird in Texas and Donna sold her 1969 Buick and drove my Thunderbird instead.

By May of 1971 an opening at Continental Airlines was available as secretary to the regional sales manager for Donna, so in early June as soon as school left out for the summer I took a week off from my new job and flew back to Houston. I rented the largest U-Haul truck available and loaded our bedroom set along with all our personal items such as wall hangings sheets blankets dishes and cookware, clothing etc. We hooked up the Thunderbird behind the U-Haul and away we went on our way to Seattle and together again!

When we arrived in Seattle I was surprised when I collected my mail from the post office to find a letter from Philippine Airlines. I set it aside and caught up on all the other mail and saved the airline envelope until last. When I finally opened the letter from Philippine Airlines I was surprised. They were asking me for an interview that was scheduled for two days from that day's date.

Now to be perfectly honest I was not really thrilled at the salary I was earning at the John Marvin Company. In any case two days later I was at the Jet Inn at 8:45 AM for my 9:00 O'clock meeting with two gentlemen named James Caputo and the other was Ed Crame. James Caputo was a big man and he was vice president of the Americas for Philippine airlines and Ed Crame was the sales manager of PAL based in Seattle. Mr. Caputo was an intimidating character with a quick mind and an arrogant attitude. It was clear that he was in charge of the interview and Ed Crame, a Filipino, was clearly subservient to him. By close to the end of the interview I was feeling the anger welling up inside me at the arrogance of James Caputo and his line of questioning. My answers I am sure were beginning to disclose my disdain for this crude man. His last question to me was 'why would a person of your ability and background want to take 2 steps forward and three steps back to go to work for Philippine Airlines'. That did it for me! He now had "broken the camels back" in my mind. I lashed out at him and told him he must not think much of Philippine Airlines if he thinks working for them would be a step backwards for me. I told him I looked at this as a challenge and I was not ignorant to the challenges that lay ahead. I reminded him of my sales experience and my accomplishments and he ended the interview with the words 'we will let you know because there are more than 900 applicants for the job'. I was now positive that I had no chance of getting this job after my last arrogant response to Mr. Caputo's question. Once again I was disappointed because I really wanted that job and although money was never discussed at that point I really did not care that much.

Needless to say it was a tremendous surprise when the phone call I received the week following asking me when I could start working for Philippine airlines that I had been chosen as the new sales rep. Although I was thrilled to the bone at the news I reminded them that we had not yet discussed salary and Mr. Crame invited me to his office the following day for that discussion.

The next day he asked me what I wanted and I told him. His offer was less and I bulked. He said he would call Mr. Caputo and see if he could meet me half way. Later, that same day Mr. Crame called me back and agreed to pay what I asked for. I had won! I gave the John Marvin Company the two week notice I felt was fair and two weeks later I was in my new office at 1400 4th avenue Bldg, 7th floor. Over the next few years I found myself on many familiarization trips to the orient and SE Asia. Ed Crame (my boss) was transferred to Australia and I was promoted to sales manager of the Pacific N.W. James Caputo and I became very good friends and we always shared a mutual respect. This is how I found myself and family in the Pacific N.W. It was the country of my dreams and I loved it dearly.

CHAPTER 18

Hunting in the Pacific NW

Having been an outdoors type person all my life I was living a "dream come true" in the Pacific NW. I have always enjoyed fishing and hunting. Since my days in Northwestern Ontario as a youngster I have hunted with a bow and arrow. Now, living in Washington State the opportunities for hunting and fishing had just expanded tremendously! I could not only fish for bass, both large and small mouth, but also trout, walleye, salmon, steelhead, not to mention all kinds of pan fish. The hunting opportunities were also expanded in that not just deer and bear of Pennsylvania but now I could hunt deer, including whitetail, black tail and mule deer but elk, bear, mountain goat, big horn sheep, cougar, bobcat, coyote, and an unlimited number of small game species including grouse and wild turkey.

One of the first things I did was invest in a whole new array of fishing gear designed specifically for steelhead fishing. New rod, reel, line, lead string, surgical tubing lures floats etc. I spent hours fishing in the Green River Gorge, using all this newly purchased equipment but failed to connect with the elusive steelhead. After about a dozen trips to the river with the same results, my patience finally came to an abrupt end and I threw my rod, reel, surgical tubing lead string and lures into the green river and decided I would focus on bass, trout and walleye instead. Thank goodness my luck in those attempts proved more successful.

Then fall arrived and deer hunting season opened along with elk season. I had read about a small island just off the mainland in southern Washington called Long Island. This island is surrounded by salt water and subject to the rise and fall of tidal surges. It was inhabited by large numbers of black tail deer as well as elk and bear so that was my first bow hunting destination. I had purchased a small boat with an outboard motor, so off to long island I went. I packed a small tent, cookstove, all the required cooking utensils, sleeping bag and food into the boat for a 5 day stay on the island. It took me just 2 days of hunting when I was successful in harvesting a nice fat black tail buck with three points on either side. Then as I was packing up my boat with all my gear and my prize buck I heard a twig snap behind me and when I spun around to see what it was, there stood a huge cow elk, staring at me as though I owed her money! My bow was already packed along with other gear in my boat, so all I could do was watch as she snorted and trotted away.

I also learned there was a healthy number of bear on this small island of seven miles long and one and a half miles wide. Almost everywhere I went I came across bear scat and I was close enough to smell them on more than one occasion. It was a wonderful place for hunting and it was restricted to bow hunters only. An added advantage for me in particular was the fact the only way onto the island was by boat and not every bow hunter had a boat. You also had to get on the island at high tide as there was just one deep channnel that was navigable at low tide but that canal was surrounded on both sides by deep mud flats that would swallow anyone or anything. I hunted there many times over the following years and harvested not just deer but a nice cow elk, a small bull elk and a boar bear of approximately 400 pounds.

One of the features of this island is the cedar grove on the southeast side. There are old growth cedars there that are more than 2000 years old! When you consider those trees are older than Jesus Christ it inspires awe and I was always humbled when I was in that grove of trees. I pray they are never harvested and I am thankful to have had the experience of seeing them in person.

My hunting grounds over the first number of years in the northwest covered area's from Long Island, Forks, Pe Ell, Enumclaw, Buckley, Kapowsin, Curlew, Thorpe, Ellensburg, Wenatchee and Othello. I have also hunted the state of Oregon on several occasions as well as Montana. As I grew older my hunting grounds focused more in the Curlew area and I became very fond of the land in that part of the country. I have seen signs of grizzly bear there as well as wolf tracks. There are big horn sheep and moose in that area as well large numbers of cougar. I also especially enjoy shooting grouse and there is no better meal than freshly harvested grouse breast, smothered in fresh mushroom sauce! I harvest all my grouse with the bow and arrow as well as wild turkey.

CHAPTER 19

Life on a yacht, the "Kitnayaqwa"

Donna and I had lived in the Seattle area for a couple years when I got the idea I would like to live on a boat. After all, if there is any place in the world to live on a boat Seattle would be that place. There is water almost every place you look. Many people live on board boats in the Pacific NW from Oregon to British Columbia. When I approached Donna about this subject she too thought it was a great idea so I went searching for the boat of my dreams. The year was 1972 and I finally found a boat that was big enough but needed a lot of work. It was an old vintage boat made of wood and it originated from a boat yard in Vancouver British Columbia. It was built in 1927. She was built of yellow cedar planking and she was owned originally by a man named Roy Umstead a Seattle police officer. Although I did not know the history of this 48 foot boat when I purchased her, I sure did like her lines but the work that was needed to make her livable was unbelievable. Never the less a young man never shies away from hard work when it comes to fulfilling his dream.

The boat was basically built in three separate cabins. There was the bow section which housed a "V" birth for sleeping and a small clothes closet. Then it was up a short flight of stairs to the wheel house. The wheel house was a nightmare!!! This vessel was powered by twin engines. The ships wheel (the helm) was on the left side but the clutch's and accelerators were on the right side of the wheel house. Access to the forward bow area was between the clutches, accelerators and the ships wheel. That had to be changed if I was going to purchase this boat.

The last thing I had to do before buying the boat was to have it surveyed by a professional ship surveyor. That required a complete dry docking and I had the boat delivered to the Seattle ship building dry docks for that purpose.

The surveyor found three 10 foot lengths of planks that needed replacement and the repair crew was hired for that purpose. It took two weeks and I finalized the purchase the day the repairs began. During those two weeks I began tearing the interior of the boat apart. At the very rear of the boat was a small cockpit for sitting while fishing and there was a doorway on the port side which opened into the main salon. My first job was to tear the rear bulkhead completely out of the boat exposing the salon to the elements. It had to be done as there was something under the floor of the main cabin that had to be removed. The floor of the main cabin was just 4 feet from the ceiling for some reason and it had to be removed if this boat was going to be livable. I was not yet aware that this boat was built for the purpose of transporting booze from Canada to the U.S. During prohibition. Nor was I aware the original engines were Liberty 12 cylinder aircraft engines which moved this boat along at 50 knots per hour, an unbelievable speed for a boat of this size in the late 20's.

After removing the rear bulkhead and the false floor of the rear cabin I found a huge steel tank about two feet high almost the complete width of the boat and the the whole length of the main cabin. It was bolted to the wood runners in the bilge and after removing the bolts that anchored it to the bilge I was able to pry it upwards several inches using a crow bar.

I had to remove this tank from the boat and I still did not know the purpose of this tank. It had no smell of gasoline or diesel. I went to the lumber yard in Ballard and purchased a couple of 8 foot 4X4 posts. Laying one end of those posts on the bottom of the bilge and the other end on top of the transom I had constructed a ramp in which I could slide this huge tank over the side.

My boat was now repaired and back in the water but it was leaking fiercely as the new planks that had been replaced needed to swell and the ship yard would not release me until they were assured the boat was no longer leaking. On a peaceful Sunday morning very early I awoke and decided this was the day to "deep six" the tank. I took an axe and cut holes on all four sides and top and with strength I didn't know I possessed I was able to move the tank up the ramp across the transom and into the water. It made a huge splash as it hit the water and the water boiled for what seemed like hours after it sank to the bottom. No one had seen me and I was crossing my fingers it would not be discovered that I had laid this huge tank on the bottom of the ship canal. I now had a 20 foot main cabin the full width of the boat on which to build my salon. The galley was just forward of the salon and the head (toilet and tub/shower) was across from the galley. Then it was up a small flight of stairs to the wheel house.

The first thing I did was to fasten a floor above the bilge the full length and width of the salon and laid champagne colored carpeting across the floor and wrapped it up the sides on both sides of salon. I had replaced the rear bulkhead with double doors in the center of the bulkhead leading out to the rear cockpit. I wired in two carriage style lights outside the double doors for 12 volt lights. I then purchased a sofa/hidabed and I had two end tables made to fit on either side of the sofa. I re-plumbed the water lines in the galley and installed a 35 gallon water heater between and aft of the two Chrysler Crown engines in the engine room. My boat, originally named "Kitnayaqua" was now back at my moorage at McGinnis Marina. My next project was the wheel house. Incidentally, the name "Kitnayaqwa" I learned later was an Indian name meaning "still running water".

The first thing I did in the wheel house was tear out the controls that were a complete disaster to operate with the wheel being on the port side and the clutches and accelerators on the starboard side. I then tore out the bulkhead between the wheel house and the forward cabin with the "V" birth. I built a new bulkhead with the stairs going down into the forward cabin on the very starboard side. I then built the instrument panel and wheel in the center of the bulkhead and the clutches and accelerators flanking both sides of the instrument panel. I installed all new instruments from RPM Tachometers, engine temp, oil pressure plus switches for anchor light, running lights, and wheel house lights. I had a tiny red light beside each switch to indicate if the light was on or not. I also had three way switches for three bilge pumps. ("on", "off" and "automatic"). If I had the switch set on automatic the red light would light up any time the pump would come on alerting me we were taking on water. If I manually turned the pump on the light would go on and stay on.

After a complete engine tune up I was ready for the maiden voyage.

On a miserable and windy, rainy Saturday morning my wife and I departed our moorage for the shakedown cruise. What an experience we were in for. I decided we should go out the locks into Puget Sound for this first cruise and so we did. Donna turned out to be a natural born sea person! Going through the locks the first time I was impressed with the way she handled the lines at the stern of the boat as I took control of the forward lines. We headed north for a couple hours, cruising at a speed of roughly 12 knots. (15 MPH). The "Kitnayaqwa" was a long and narrow vessel and was built for speed and not so much for comfort. I did not notice the rising wind coming out of the south and the following sea that had been building for some time. We were approaching Rosario straits when I decided we had gone far enough, and I was in for a sobering surprise when I went to make a turn to head south. The swells were now about 6 feet and I had to turn broadside to regain a southward direction. With a 48 foot boat and a 10 foot width, it was going to be a real rocking experience to accomplish this move. I was sitting comfortably in my lavish captain's chair and Donna was standing by my side with a good grip on the side of the instrument panel. I was watching aft for a wave that was lower than the rest, to make my move but after a long wait decided none were coming so I committed to the turn and made a hard turn to port. I increased the RPM's of my starboard engine to make the turn more quickly but knew we were in for a dangerous rolling experience. Once I was broadside to the following sea the full impact of the giant swells coupled with the high winds out of the south the "Kitnayaqua" nearly broached as it struggled to regain its southward heading! Once we were straightened out on a southward course with the waves now breaking over our bow I glanced over at Donna. She was white as a sheet and wanting to put her mind as ease, I said "this sure gives you faith in this old boat doesn't it" and she replied "no, this gives you faith in God"!!!

I looked down at my instrument panel and all were normal but two of the three bilge pump lights were glowing red. I wanted more than anything to open the hatch to the engine room to see how much water I was dealing with but I knew I could not leave the wheel for a second. Hopefully Donna would not notice the lights.

2 hours and 45 minutes later we were once again in calm waters approaching the Ballard locks to again get raised into fresh water and home at McGinnis Marina. My bilge pump lights were still on and I was still anxious to see how much water I was dealing with in the bilge. It had to wait until I was back in my slip and re-hooked to shore power and water etc.

Finally I was able to open the engine room hatch and look into the bilge. To my great relief there were just an inch or so of water in the bilge and I could hear the pump humming as it was doing its job of draining my bilge of water. I then checked the aft cockpit bilge and it was completely dry. I finally went to the forward cabin bilge and it too was humming away and had just a few inches of water.

For the following two weeks the bilge pumps ran periodically but less frequently every day until the planking again reseated and became water tight once again. The "Kitnayaqwa" suffered some very severe twisting and pounding as we were bounced over the huge swells of a Puget Sound storm. Next time I made it a point to listen to the weather channel prior to taking a leisurely cruise.

Living on board a boat is the most satisfying experience a person who loves the water could ever want or dream of. After a long week of the rat race of corporate life there is nothing more relaxing that unplugging the telephone, electricity and water and spending the weekend on Puget Sound exploring new inlets and islands. Salmon fishing was also on my list of favorite things to do and I became very good at that over the following years. I learned at what depth of water you were most likely to encounter salmon and I also learned where they loved to hang out. I practiced the catch and release program and usually just kept one for eating purposes.

I do have a very fond memory of a vacation Donna and I took on our boat one summer. We were in northern Puget Sound nearing the Canadian border and there were two uninhabited islands named Suscia and the other was Macia. On the north side of Macia was a secluded and protected cove where we would anchor for the nights but the north side of Suscia was rather dangerous as there was a reef just under the surface of the water that could not be seen but could rip the bottom out of any boat. When tide was changing the water would rush through the gap between the reef and the island, stirring up any bait fish that might be there and there always were some. The secret to catching salmon in that area was simple. Just cruise against the tide until you cleared the gap between the reef and the island and turn 180 degrees and drift back through the gap with the tide while trolling a flasher with a rubber squid of various colors. You would catch a salmon every time you did that! They ranged from 35 to 70 pounds. My lovely wife Donna would usually run the boat while I did all the fishing but on this one occassion she insisted she wanted to read a book! I had two pole holders in the aft cockpit, one on the port side and one on the starboard. There were windows on all sides of the wheel house so I could sit sideways on my captain's seat (which swiveled) and have a clear view both fore and aft. So Donna went to the rear cockpit and settled in for a read while I was left with the chore of running the boat and watching the rod tips as well as keeping the boat between the reef and the island. I had a public address system on the boat that was part of my ship to shore radio/telephone and when I looked aft I saw the port fishing rod bouncing up and down like crazy!!! I grabbed the "mic" and yelled "FISH ON" and Donna being inexperienced with catching fish was taking way too long to put her book down and grab the jumping rod. I leaped from the captain's chair and sped through the salon to the cockpit door not even giving a second thought what could happen to my precious boat if it were to touch the reef or the rocks of the island. I reached for the rod that Donna was now holding with a fighting large salmon on the other end and was totally surprised to hear her yell "get away, this is my fish"! She had never shown any interest in fishing before. Obediently I grabbed the net in preparation of landing a huge salmon because I could tell from the bending of the rod this was not a juvenile salmon! Donna was doing a terrific job for a person that had never caught a fish before and after another 20 minutes the huge fish was approaching the Kitnayaqwa. Just as the huge fish was coming to the surface to be netted I could clearly see the blue and white rubber squid hanging from the corner of its mouth. At the same instant I saw an even larger salmon trying his best to eat the part of the squid that was hanging out of the corner of the hooked salmon's mouth! In a quick swoop I swung the net into the water encompassing what I thought would be two salmon. To my disappointment I came up with just one 54 pound salmon in my net as the second one must have seen the net hit the water and sped off in an instant. I honestly believe the second salmon (compared to the size of the 54 pounder) would have been upwards of 75 pounds. Donna was hooked on salmon fishing from that day forward.

You have heard the prayer of many a sailor that goes something like this. "Oh Lord, thy ocean is so large and my boat is so small"? Well, believe me I have said that prayer more than once. On one occasion my three small children were visiting me for a two week vacation on the "Kitnayaqwa". We had left the confines of my slip at McGinnis Marina and had been cruising on the huge expanse of Puget Sound from Seattle north. We had fished most days and anchored every night with my crap pots set out to do their job catching Dungeness crabs as we slept.

In the mornings I was busy separating the female crabs and returning them to the Sound as only the males are legal to keep. Then I would cook them up and clean them and there is nothing better than freshly caught crab meat. We were again in northern Puget Sound and anchored at my favorite cove behind Macia Island. My kids were starving from a long day of fishing and I was busy cleaning salmon when a small power boat with two guys in scuba gear came slowly into the cove where we were anchored. I was back on my swim platform cleaning the salmon and one of the fellows asked politely if I would be willing to trade one of my salmon for a bunch of fresh scallops. I said, 'of course but you don't need to sacrifice any of your hard earned scallops for a salmon'. They seemed like two very nice young men and I asked them if they would like to join us for dinner. They said they would like that very much so I lowered my skiff and took all the food Donna had prepared for dinner and went ashore on Macia Island. Shortly we had a nice fire going in a quickly made fire pit and Donna had prepared the salmon for baking and it was wrapped in tin foil and a pot of boiling and seasoned water was ready for the scallops. Someone had the idea of the same thing we were doing sometime prior to our arrival because there was a picnic table nearby and soon our new friends were sitting around the campfire enjoying Potato salad, salmon and scallops along with a tossed salad, ice cold beer for the adults and Pop for the kids. We sat around the campfire for a few hours, watching the stars and eventually our friends bid farewell and we returned to the "Kitnayaqwa" for a good night's sleep.

Our two week vacation in the San Juan Islands of Puget Sound was fast coming to the end and it was time we began our two day cruise back to the Seattle area.

After raising anchor and saying goodbye to Macia Island we turned south for our next destination of Friday Harbor. As we slowly pulled into the Harbor area we could clearly see that all the available slips were occupied so we dropped anchor in the harbor and prepared to spend the night anchored in the harbor waters. There was a huge 120 foot yacht anchored some distance away and I suddenly recognized it as the "Wild Goose"! For those not familiar with the yacht 'Wild Goose' that yacht is owned by non-other than John (the duke) Wayne the Hollywood movie star. He loved the Puget Sound waters and his visits were an annual affair. His yacht was a converted mine sweeper from WWII and made into a beautiful, livable yacht. My children were very young at the time with Sandy, the oldest, being 9 years old and Steve the youngest being just six years old. Sherry was 8 years of age. My kids were all standing around in the wheel house and I said 'do you know who owns that big boat over there' and when they said they didn't I said that boat belongs to John Wayne! Sherry almost flipped her lid! She said 'Dad, you have to put the dingy in the water and let me go over there'. I thought about it for a minute and finally agreed to lower the dingy. Sherry was born with a very high IQ and her wit is unmatched. I shuddered to think what she would say when John Wayne appeared on deck to talk to her. I watched from the wheel house as she and Steve paddled their way across the couple hundred yards to the "Wild Goose". I picked up my binoculars and watched as she approached the big yacht and pulled alongside. She stood up and was knocking on the hull of the big boat and I saw a gentleman open the salon door and come on deck. He leaned over the side and looked down at my daughter and I watched as they were obviously in deep conversation. Sherry was making hand gestures and the man (not John Wayne) was throwing his arms in the air in frustration. I could only imagine what was being said and I was afraid to find out. Finally the man walked back inside and Sherry was paddling her way back to the "Kitnayaqwa". When she finished tieing up the dingy and coming back on board she told me what had occurred. John Wayne was at the Eagles club in town and the man that answered the knocking from Sherry was not allowed to give her a photo of John Wayne without his permission. Sherry was upset! I set out the crab pot for more crab meat and we spent a relaxing day just laying around and enjoying the beautiful sunshine of the Pacific NW. I told Sherry she could try again tomorrow to see John Wayne and she finally settled down.

The following morning I was up at 4 AM to pull up my crab pot and prepare to begin the cruise back to my slip at McGinnis Marine. I was not going to leave until Sherry had one more chance to see John Wayne but just at 6 o'clock AM I looked over towards the Wild Goose and I saw the anchor being raised as John Wayne himself was sauntering on the deck in that typical signature walk he is so famous for. I quickly woke Sherry so she could at least get a glimpse of him as he strode the deck of the Wild Goose. Now she was really mad! Slowly the Wild Goose turned south and soon disappeared from sight.

After breakfast we too raised anchor and turned south for our trip to Seattle. By midafternoon we were almost 20 miles from the Ballard locks. Everyone was sleeping. I always had my captain's chair swiveled sideways so I could look ahead or aft. When looking forward I saw a great distance away something sticking out of the water dead ahead. I reminded myself to keep an eye on that object as it could be a dead head (log just under the surface). Several minutes later I again looked forward to see that object but it had disappeared. I grabbed my binoculars because now I was worried as I did not want to hit a submerged log. When I finally focused the binoculars I again saw the object sticking straight up and it was a lot closer. Suddenly there appeared another object sticking straight up and then another. Killer whales!, I yelled, and all three children came running up to the wheel house. I passed right through a pod of killer whales with several on my port side and several on my starboard. One big male came very close and spy hopped right next to my wheel house door which was open. I could clearly see his blood shot eye as he peered into the wheel house! I am so very thankful those huge beasts do not get angry with us because if they just tapped our boat with their huge bodies they would sink us on the spot. My children's dream of seeing a Killer Whale was fulfilled and all were satisfied except for Sherry, who never got to meet John Wayne.

Before long, the entrance to the Ballard locks was coming into view and as we got closer I peered over toward the Shilshole Bay Marina. There tied to the guest pier was the Wild Goose. I yelled for Sherry and she came running! "There is the Wild Goose" I said, and she said "Dad you have to take me over there". I promised I would as soon as we got back into my slip and tied up.

Finally everything was done and the boat was now back on shore power, shore water and telephone hookups. I loaded Sherry into the car and drove the short distance to the Shilshole Bay Marina. I parked in front of the pier that led to the end of the guest dock and the Wild Goose that was tied up there. Again I watched as Sherry ran as fast as her legs could carry her and once again she knocked on the hull of the big yacht. I watched in horror as John Wayne came to the door and I could clearly see Sherry shaking her finger at him and she must have been yelling something. I saw her waving her arms and pointing north and then to my car and finally john Wayne turned and stepped back inside. Sherry turned towards the car and I could see a huge smile on her face and I was not sure if I should be embarrassed or happy for her. When I looked back John Wayne was again standing in front of Sherry looking down and he was writing something on what he was holding in his hands. Then I saw him reach down and pick her up and give her a big kiss and set her back down gently on the dock! As she ran back to my car holding some papers in her hands I saw John Wayne as he looked at me and waved before disappearing again inside his huge yacht.

John "Duke" Wayne had given Sherry not one photo of himself but one for Sandy and Steve as well. The Photo was of him on a big sorrel horse wearing a patch on one eye as he looked when filming "True Grit". He autographed each photo with all three names of my children, one on each photo. What a gentleman he was!!!

The following day was a sad day as I watched my three children board the plane for the flight back to Pennsylvania. It was a memorable vacation that will never be forgotten.

CHAPTER 20

The Kitnayaqwa, vintage yacht

Donna and I both worked hard and we had gotten into the habit of "eating out" several times a week. There were lots of restaurants located on the shores of Lake Union as well as Lake Washington. We would come home from work tired and hungry and not wanting Donna to have to cook dinner after a long and tiring day I would suggest that we cruise to the lake and have dinner at one of the lakeside restaurants. She always agreed and away we went in our floating home and we would dock and tie up at any one of the many excellent restaurants.

As I mentioned in an earlier chapter, the original engines in the "Kitnayaqwa" were 12 cylinder aircraft engines. The stringers in the engine room were proof that at one time there were massive engines mounted on them. (stringers are beams that marine engines are mounted to). My stringers were a massive 6 inches wide and 18 inches tall and there were two for each engine. The keelson, or center beam, of the Kitnayaqwa was a solid oak beam, 12 inches wide by 12 inches deep and reached the entire length of the boat. The two tiny Chrysler crowns sitting between these massive stringers was a sight to see but made working on the engines very easy. Unfortunately when the Chrysler engines were installed, replacing the aircraft engines they were installed on the wrong sides.

With twin engine boats the engines must turn in opposite directions for the boat to operate correctly. The rotation of the propellers is always turning outwards to the side the motor was mounted on. These engines were mounted so the rotation was turning inwards for some unknown reason. The "Kitnayaqwa" had no keel. (that is the plate that on most boats extends downward in the center of the bottom of the boat). The "kitnayaqwa instead had a keelson which is the beam I described earlier that is all on the inside of the hull and not protruding downward from the center of the boat. The accidental benefit of this installation error was that with proper maneuvering of the clutches and rudders the boat could move sideways in close quarters as though it had bow thrusters. Over the months of operating the Kitnayaqwa I learned how to "park" her almost anywhere that would have been impossible for any other boat.

Such was the case that evening as Donna and I pulled into the secluded docking area of the "Hungry Turtle Restaurant". It was winter time and the days were short so it was already dark as I docked and tied up.

We made our way to the entrance and were escorted to our table. We had just taken our seats when we were approached by a gentleman who introduced himself as a writer for the Seattle Post Intelligencer news paper, Mr. Jack Williams. He asked if I was the skipper that just brought that big yacht into the restaurant dock. When I told him I was, he asked if he could have the honor of having a closer look at her after dinner. I told him of course and he returned to his table and we ordered our dinner. He may have finished his meal before us but he patiently waited for Donna and I to finish ours and after paying our bill we escorted Mr. Williams to the "Kitnayaqwa". He almost could not contain himself with excitement as he walked through the wheel house and down the stairs into the salon. He kept repeating over and over again "what a ship" what a ship"! We sat for a few minutes and he then told me he knew of this boat called the Kitnayaqwa and it had quite a history. He asked if he could write an article on her and put it on the front page of the Sunday paper the following weekend. He also said that he wanted a photo of her and we arranged for a time that I could take the Kitnayaqwa from her covered slip to the end of our moorage for a photo.

As promised the following Sunday I went out and bought the Sunday paper and sure enough there I was on the front page of the Seattle Post Intellegencer. This is what I learned from his article.

The Kitnayaqwa was built in 1927 (which I already knew) but was not christened until 1929. She was built and paid for by a Seattle police officer named Roy Umstead, for the sole purpose of running booze from Vancouver, British Columbia to Seattle during prohibition, a totally illegal enterprise. The kitnayaqwa not only had those huge aircraft engines that sped her along at 50 knots per hour, an unbelievable speed for that year in our history but she ran these waters at night time in total darkness. Since the wheel house was forward of amidships and the engines were under the wheel house there were a series of mufflers that ran the length of the boat, deadened the roar of those gigantic engines. All throughout the prohibition years Mr. Umstead would make a quick run to Canada to pick up a tank full of bulk booze and return with it, sliding his big boat under the piers at low tide to unload and bottle the liquid gold!

Just before the law was changed allowing the sale of alcoholic beverages to be sold in America Mr. Umstead was finally arrested. He was sentenced to 20 years in the McNeal Island Penitentiary. It left a scar on the Seattle police force that lasted for years and Mr. Umstead I am told died at the McNeal Island Penitentiary some years later. The US government had built a very fast boat themselves in an effort to catch the rum running boats. There was evidence when my boat was being repaired at time of purchase, that she indeed took a shell from a 50 caliber machine gun. The chase boats that were owed by the U.S. Government had bow mounted 50 caliber machine guns. The hole had been packed with oakum and sealed using a lead plug was the same size as a projectile from a 50 caliber projectile. It was at the waterline and was one of the planks that were replaced at the time I purchased the vessel. To this day it is not clear if the Kitnayaqwa was ever captured. The suspicious lead plug packed with oakum was the only evidence there may have been an arrest of the boat itself. Mr. Umstead was arrested but no record of the boat being seized was ever found.

CHAPTER 21

Hershel, the Sea Lion

I t was 1979 or 1980 when a sea lion named "Hershel", by the local media, became famous. Salmon that were hatched in fresh water streams, made their way down stream to ocean waters, only to return to the exact stream they were hatched, to spawn and die three years later. Millions of these salmon enter fresh water by entering the Ballard locks every year as fully grown sockeye, humpback, king and silver salmon. Full of eggs they make their way through all kinds of hazards, fighting their way upstream to the place of their birth. This mass congregation of salmon apparently caught the attention of a huge sea lion and looking for an easy meal he too entered the spillway of the Ballard locks which is a ship channel leading to the locks. In the late summer months vast numbers of spectators gather at the locks on weekends to watch as boats of all shapes and sizes return from a weekend on Puget Sound. It was on one such weekend the spectators were in for a bonus as Hershel made his debut and the great salmon massacre began.

This giant sea lion weighed well over one thousand pounds and he was killing hundreds of salmon per day. It wasn't long before a few of his female friends joined him in his murderous venture. As days passed both the Seattle Times News and the Seattle P. I. were printing front page stories of the great salmon massacre occurring at the Ballard locks. The fisheries department was trying everything in their arsenal to defer the activities of Hershel and his friends but nothing seemed to work. They used rubber bullets fired from shotguns but they just bounced off the huge beasts and were nothing more than a mosquito bite to the sea lions. They tried catching them in cages but were out smarted by the pesky sea creatures. Then they used giant nets but the sea lions figured out how to jump over the net just before it closed in on them.

By this time the sea lions were killing thousands of salmon per day because they were just taking a bite out of each salmon and eating the tasty salmon roe. The poor, fatally wounded salmon were in for a slow death and doomed to become crab food. As more time passed the sea lions became even more brazen and were now coming into the locks and up into the fresh water, some 18 feet higher than the sea level of Puget Sound. The moorage where my yacht, the "Kitnayaqwa" was tied up was just inside the fresh water side of the Ballard locks on the city of Ballard side of the ship canal. It was a covered moorage with dozens of other yachts moored there as well.

During the summer when we were enjoying a nice relaxing weekend without taking our boat out of our moorage we would have a dock party and all those living on their boats would join in. It was on one such occasion when we were all sitting around drinking the cocktail of our choice when we heard the now familiar "ARF-ARF-ARF" of Hershel the big male sea lion. He was close and I got up to see exactly where he was. The Marina where we were moored called McGinnis Marina had two long piers. One pier was covered moorage and the other was not covered. As I neared the end of our pier I saw this huge sea lion Hershel lying on the end of the dock on the uncovered pier. I walked back to the party and told my friends where Hershel was. Jim Heuther, one of my friends said "Merrill, you should take your bow and arrow and shoot him"! It is amazing how a person's judgment changes with the amount of alcohol consumed and suddenly that seemed like a good idea! I have hunted with a bow and arrow my entire life and over the years I have harvested many deer, bear, elk as well as various small game species. The arrows I shoot are all cut to the length of my draw and are matched equally. I also had a few arrows that I have found in the woods while hunting that did not belong to me and were no match to any arrow I owned. Most of these arrows were longer than my arrows, some of which were several inches longer. I was a deadly shot with a bow and rightfully so with all the experience I had over the years. I could hit the bull's eye on targets from 10 yards to 60 yards in those days. All these things were spinning through my mind as I sat back down in my chair as the dock party continued. Jim again said 'you should shoot him Merrill' and I replied 'give me another martini'! I knew it was illegal to shoot a sea lion as they are protected by law. I also thought about how much I loved salmon fishing. Then I thought about all the people I knew that enjoyed salmon fishing. I thought about all the thousands of salmon that would not be alive for me to catch because of the murderous escapades of Hershel and his friends. I visualized in my mind the hero status I would enjoy even being anonymous by all the fishermen in the northwest if I were to eliminate Hershel. Another martini would definitely be a good thing right now so I had another.

Without saying a word I got up, went into our boat and grabbed my bow, one of the arrows that did not belong to me and my range finder. I could not miss my target (the heart) of this giant beast. It had to be a quick and silent death because I surely did not want to be caught killing this scourge of salmon death.

I stopped just before reaching the end of our covered pier and stood there in the shadow as I laid my bow and lone arrow on the dock. I was ranging the distance between myself and the soon to be expired Hershel when I heard footsteps on the dock coming towards me. I looked away from my range finder to see "Bud" McGinnis, the owner of the marina walking toward me! He obviously saw my bow and arrow lying on the dock at my feet and he had also seen me looking through my range finder. He said 'you are not going to shoot him are you' and before his last word was out of his mouth I replied 'oh hell no, I was just taking pictures! I was hoping he thought my range finder was a camera.

I sheepishly picked up my bow and arrow and made my way back to my boat to put everything back where it belonged. No one said a word and I had another martini.

The following morning I awoke with not just a hangover but also relief that I had not killed Hershel for I surely would have been caught and charged with a felony. Might still be in jail to this day!

CHAPTER 22

First trip to Communist China

February of 1977 found me on my way to Hong Kong on Philippine airlines with stops in Honolulu and Manila, with the ultimate destination after Hong Kong being communist China. I was escorting 29 American travel agents on a familiarization tour of the Orient and China. We had a few days in Manila for sightseeing and R&R before we headed for Hong Kong, our jumping off point into the previously forbidden country of China. Philippine Airlines was the first international Airlines to achieve the 'Fifth Freedom Right' of travel to mainland China. That means that an agreement was signed between authorities of both countries to allow their individual airlines the privilege of flying into and landing in the reciprocal country. CAAC (which stands for the Civil Aeronautics Association of China) was then allowed to fly into and land in the country of the Philippine's and PAL, (Philippine Airlines) was allowed to fly into and land in the country of China.

I was extremely fortunate as I was the first tourist group (regular people) to enter this country since President Nixon had opened the door to China a few years prior. The first people that were invited into China were politicians such as congressmen and senators. After all those politicians that were invited to visit China had traveled there the next invited guests were Hollywood movie stars that had never performed in a movie that had never shed any bad light on China. When all the movie stars that were invited to visit China were exhausted the first American regular people (tourists) were allowed to enter. Kind of humbling to know that in China's eyes I was a simple 'regular' person

When we left the Philippines we also left the tropical climate and the 80 to 90 degree temperatures we had just enjoyed there.

Hong Kong was a bit colder and the temperature there was in the high 50's to low 60's for that time of the year. Our journey into China was going to be a 21 day prearranged tour that only Chinese officials knew the itinerary of. My group of travel agents were all seasoned travelers and I had 30 copies of the group visa which I carried in my attaché case. I also took control of all of my group members passports before we left the United States and they too were stuffed away in my attaché case along with all their airline tickets.

To my surprise we were not to fly into China from Hong Kong but we boarded a 1920 vintage steam locomotive and that was the only choice of rail travel the Chinese had for us since they did not yet have diesel engines. It did not take long after leaving the New Territories of Hong Kong to cross the border into this new and unexplored (by US citizens) country of communist China. I must admit that although I was acting as the tour director for this trip, it was actually the "blind leading the blind". I had never been to China before. There was no reading material available to familiarize one's self of things to come. We all were just along for the ride. It was amazing to look out the window of the moving train and see the poverty. The poor living standards of the residents of China were evident as the train sped past the rice fields and villages along the way. Prior to taking this trip I was given a list of names of the 29 people that were joining me on this trip as well as their addresses. I had contacted each and every one of them and advised them to be sure to bring a month's supply of cigarettes and booze if they enjoyed a drink after a long day and a cigarette from time to time. American booze and cigarettes were not available in China and I was told that by our PAL management team before we left the states. I had several memorable persons on board this trip and one of those persons was a lady named Harriet Price! She indeed was priceless and I shall never forget her. Although she did not drink or smoke she did carry the world's largest purse! She was an older woman, heavy set with a sense of humor unmatched by anyone. It wasn't until later in the trip that I finally understood the reason for the large purse. Another person that I remember well was a younger man with the name of Bruce Burcham. Now Bruce was gay but he too was a joy to have on the trip as he was always laughing, even when we had little if anything to laugh at. As we all learned later, during this trip, he was born a twin and was the second of the two to see the light of day. For that reason I dubbed him with the nickname of "BB" Burcham. (the second "B" meaning "beta", the second to be born). He got a big "kick" out of being named that and everyone enjoyed his company. Then we had a gentleman and his wife along and their names were George and Joan Stoner. They owned a travel agency in Gig Harbor, Washington and he was also a weekend warrior, meaning he was in the U. S. Coast Guard reserves. As it turned out he was a royal pain in the neck throughout the entire trip and if I could have sent him home from China I surely would have. No one liked him after about the third day and they did not like his wife either. All in all it was a good group of people and I did my best to keep George Stoner and his wife, under control.

Our first stop was in the city of Guangzhou, formally known as Canton. Before I go much further I must tell you something about the Chinese people. When they decided to open the doors to the world for the first time they also knew they would need some high rise hotels to accommodate these visitors. They did have a few hotels that were five and 6 stories tall but they had been built in the 20's and 30's or before the turn of the century. So they began building new high rise hotels for the guests they were expecting. The Pink Swan Hotel was one of these new high rise hotels and had just recently been finished and was waiting for our arrival in Canton (now called Quangzhou). When we arrived at the train station in Canton we were met by a local guide named Chung Ching Kuo. He had studied English and could speak our language very well indeed. He escorted my group and me to the waiting bus for our ride to this new hotel, the Pink Swan. He spoke on the microphone to my group and gave us a short orientation of our next 3 days in Guangzhou. He also advised me that upon arrival at the Pink Swan he needed to see me either in the bar or in my room for what he called "consultation". I agreed to meet him in my room.

After receiving all the keys and distributing them to the group members Chung and I headed for my room. The meeting lasted for about 45 minutes and it consisted of expected protocol from me as tour director when meeting heads of state, politicians, heads of communes etc. Being the tour leader meant that only I could speak to their leaders and any questions by members of my group had to be addressed to me and I in turn had to ask the head of whatever organization we were visiting through my interpreter, Chung Ching Kuo. My group members were not allowed to ask any questions without going through me. I would ask the leader the question he would give me the answer (through the interpreter) and I would relay that info on to the group member that asked the question. Why they insisted on this procedure I will never know but several years went by before they finally dropped that protocol. Everyone but guess who respected that rule and that finally came to a head when we were visiting one of China's most successful communes. (you guessed it, George Stoner). He came very close to having us all thrown out of China! I had to apologize profusely to the commune leader and then I was asked by the commune leader to publicly denounce and belittle George Stoner in front of all the guests that were invited to a dinner banquet that was being held in honor of my group that evening. I must confess that I looked forward to that coming event with great pleasure! Chung and I sat in my room for a couple hours while I wrote a reprimand to George Stoner that would have made the late Chairman Mao proud! George Stoner is the perfect example as to why travelling Americans are sometimes referred to as 'Ugly Americans'. My entire group was embarrassed by his behavior as well as his wife's behavior.

The banquet that evening was something to behold!!!! We were all ushered into a giant hall with high ceilings and tall windows and this room could easily accommodate one thousand people. Although there were just 29 people in my group the tables were set for about 50 and all 50 chairs were filled. They had the local head of state who sat next to my interpreter and I sat on the other side of the interpreter. There was the mayor of the village commune as well as chief of police and several military personnel. There were many more people but they were not identified. Chung, the Head of State and I sat at the head table with Chung sitting between the Head of State and myself. Dinner service began with pre dinner drinks consisting of a horrible liquid called Mao Tai. When they uncapped the bottle, the room smelled almost instantaneously like dirty socks! It tasted worse! It was served in a shot glass and one chug and it was gone. No sooner did I empty my shot glass and it was refilled for the next round of toasts. The head of state toasted me. I then toasted the Head of State. He would ask if my parents were still living and when I replied 'yes they were' we first had to toast my father, then my mother. I returned the questions to him and of course we had to toast his dead father and his living mother. By this time my knees were going numb and my mouth was going to sleep as well so I suggested I needed to slow down a little. He said OK but we had to toast the fact that we were going to slow down!

The next surprise was the first course of our nine course dinner. Now you must know that silverware was not used in China and none of us had silverware accept Harriet Price. She had that in her purse along with whatever else she had hidden away in there. They came out with silver platters of tiny little sparrows; all cooked with their tiny little wings folded back like tiny little turkeys on Thanksgiving Day. They were all lined up like a squadron of airplanes on an aircraft carrier. For the life of me I was at a loss as to how to eat these little critters. I looked over and Harriet had her fork and knife and was having trouble slicing meat off the breast of the sparrow. Before I could ask Chung how to eat these birds I saw him pick up a bird with his chop sticks and pop the whole tiny bird in his mouth. One by one he reached to his mouth to remove a bone and after a few minutes he had the complete skeleton of the poor little sparrow sitting in a pile next to his plate including its head and beak. By then we were all following this procedure and eventually we polished off the last of the sparrows. Then came the pallet cleanser. Cucumber soaked in very strong vinegar. Our next course was fish eye soup. Each bowl of soup had at least six fish eyes staring up at us from the fish broth they were floating in. Then we had some kind of fish with the head of the fish on the plate. After that course we were fed pork of some kind but it tasted a bit like fish. (I learned later from Chung that the pigs are fed fish and that is why they taste of fish). After several more courses (one of which I am positive was snake) we finally got to the main course, Peking duck. It was good considering that all they fed us was the skin of the duck. When we finally finished the main course there were several types of desert offered if anyone had room of any more food. We all had a little desert to avoid insulting our host. The temperature in the dining room we were in was the same temperature as the outside temperature and that was in the low 50's. We were all wearing our sweaters.

After our banquet we headed back to the Pink Swan Hotel. This was a brand new high rise hotel of 30 stories tall. The outside of the hotel was painted pink and there was a beautiful water fountain and fish pool in front of the main entrance. There was large coy fish swimming in the pool under the water fountain.

We all went to my room for happy hour and everyone broke out their drink of choice. Harriet brought out a box of Ritz Crackers and a block of cheese. She then produced a cheese knife and a small paper plate and proceeded to slice cheese for everyone.

Being the tour director it was my pleasure to be given a suite instead of a regular sized room so there was more than enough room for all 29 members of my group to sit. When looking more closely at the construction of the hotel we all found it amusing when it became obvious they had installed the carpeting before plastering and painting the interior walls.

All along the edges of the room, where the carpet met the wall, there were large clumps of white dried plaster and pale blue paint splattered over the carpet. The lack of workmanship in the bathroom was even more evident as there were huge gaps between the wall and one end of the bath tub and there was paint splattered around the edges. Where the floor tile had to be cut to fit at the end of the floor near the edge of the wall, the cuts were not made square and the uneven gaps were filled with plaster or in some cases nothing at all.

Hot water was at a premium and it took upwards of ten minutes to get warm water to your bathroom shower after turning on the hot water. My group was on the 16th floor and I was on the 30th floor. When I asked why I was separated from my group they explained that was standard procedure for tour directors as it offered me a greater degree of privacy. That policy is still followed today throughout the Orient and Southeast Asia.

After a few days in Guangzhou, visiting shrines and the zoo where we saw the Giant Panda Bears, we were driven back to the train station and a 13 hour trip to our next destination, Xian. One thing I will say about the rail system in China is that the trains are always on time. When they say departure time is three O'clock PM that is exactly what they mean. Not one minute before or one minute after. The bell tower in the Guangzhou Train Station was still resonating from the third strike when the steam driven locomotive began moving out of the station. The cars were antique in American standards and made mostly of wood with large wood frame windows. There was no dining car or food service but each car had bench seats facing each other with a table between them and the tables had white linen table cloths, a large thermos of hot water, a bouquet of fresh flowers in a vase that was fastened on to the side of the car under the window. There were four China cups and saucers for the hot water and a small metal bucket filled with green tea bags. In the center of the car to one side the bench seats were missing and in their place was a potbellied coal stove. That stove became our best friend as we sped along to our destination of Xian. Xian is the place where the buried terracotta soldiers were discovered in the mid 70's.

Every hour the temperatures got colder and colder and it was not long before we began seeing snow on the ground. The conductor came by from time to time to throw another bucket of coal on the fire to keep it warm in our car. We were now speeding along at what I would estimate to be close to 60 MPH. We had no stops since we left Guangzhou so I can only assume this train was for our exclusive use. We saw no other passengers.

It must have been close to midnight and Chung, who was seated next to me asked questions about America as both he and I sipped our tea and chatted. He was so inquisitive about everything American. Questions like 'is it true that every American has two cars'? 'Is it true that all American homes have their own swimming pool? 'Is it true that American fathers beat their children'. Suddenly and without any warning the train slammed on the brakes. Our thermos bottles went flying, along with the China cups and saucers that shattered on the floor. I had no idea a moving train could stop that fast but we came to a complete stop. It was a moonlit night and I could see the snow covered ground out the window as Chung said he would find out what happened. He left our car and disappeared into the car in front of us. The lights in our car became very dim and were flickering and we sat there waiting for Chung's return. The conductor came by with a broom and pan on a long pole and was cleaning up the broken China cups and saucers. Later he returned with more China cups and saucers and fresh hot water thermos bottles.

The train started moving again when Chung re-entered our car and he was about as white as a sheet. Everyone was asking him what had happened and he kept saying "nothing important". After everyone returned to their seat he leaned towards me and revealed the purpose of our unscheduled stop. It seems that two young men had committed suicide by laying down on the tracks in front of the train. What Chung had seen was the lower half of the two bodies. The engineer had seen the two young men enter the tracks and slammed on the brakes but the train was unable to stop before slicing them in two.

We must have increased our speed for some time because at precisely four O'clock AM we slowed down as we entered the city of Xian. What a surprise we had when we exited the warm car. It had to be below zero degrees outside and there was no bus to pick us up. Chung said not to worry, he was sure the bus was on its way. It was snowing furiously and our baggage was stacked on a pile getting covered with the snow. We stood under the narrow roof which did little to protect us from the elements. Five O'clock came and went and still no bus. By this time my fingers were freezing cold and my nose was numb as my feet began to get cold as well. George Stoner was cussing the "stupid Chinese" and I went over and told him to shut his mouth. Six O'clock came and went and now our feet were numb as well and Chung was getting worried. About 20 minutes after six O'clock the bus finally arrived. We all piled into the warm bus and were off to a restaurant for something to eat! Finally!

We came to a huge building and were escorted through to a huge dining hall that was surely big enough to seat a thousand people. We sat down at this very long table and breakfast was served almost immediately. It was nearly as cold inside this restaurant as it was outside. We were served a full American style breakfast with scrambled eggs, bacon that tasted fishy and potatoes that also tasted fishy. To drink we were offered the strongest coffee I have ever tasted. It must have been brewed several times at least a month prior to our arrival. It was hot however and after the two hours we spent in the frigid outdoors waiting for the bus we drank it regardless. Our breathing left steam drifting in front of our faces but we laughed and ate our meal.

I was however stunned when I was getting towards the end of my scrambled eggs. I had to force myself to eat the bacon as it tasted more like fish than some of the fish I had already eaten in China. As I impaled my last piece of scrambled egg on my chop sticks and raised it off the plate it revealed a fried and very dead cock roach lying on my plate. Chung saw it but paid no attention to it. I waved to the waiter to come to my table and when he did I asked him in a straight face if I had to pay extra for the roach which I was pointing at. Obviously he did not speak English as he nodded and smiled before he bowed and backed away. I did eat the last of the scrambled eggs but did not eat the cock roach.

For those of you that are not familiar with the Village of Xian that happens to be the area where the buried terra cotta soldiers were uncovered under hundreds of tons of earth. We were the first group of regular American tourists to visit this discovery site and it was a very impressive experience. They had constructed a huge tent that covered the sight and very little of it had been excavated at the time we were there. We could clearly see the life sized soldiers as they were lined up in a marching position and there were horses with riders all made of terra cotta flanking either side. Every face on each soldier was different and recognizable as a separate individual. It was an incredible experience to say the least!!! We spent most of the day there inspecting the details of each and every thing we saw. The Chinese archeologists were busy uncovering more of the standing army of soldiers. These soldiers and horses were all life size and you could not help but stand in awe of the artists that made each and every one of these incredible statues! The individual faces of these soldiers were all different and unique.

After another day of sightseeing we were off again on a flight to our next destination. This time we were put on a CAAC flight to the city of Hangzhou. This too developed into a real learning experience for my group and me. When we arrived at the airport, a Quonset Hut next to a concrete air strip we saw the airplane we were about to board. It was a three engine airplane similar to our 727 aircraft that were manufactured by Boeing back in the 60's. There were hundred's of Chinese people standing there waiting to board the plane and clearly many more than the plane was capable of accommodating. We were escorted past all the Chinese people and were the first to board. It was a very unusual experience to board a plane the way we did. We walked out onto the tarmac to a pickup truck that was equipped with a fancy looking staircase built from the bed of the pickup and rose to the door of the plane when the pick-up truck was parked the way it was. Behind the pickup truck was a wooden box sitting on the ground that was our first giant step to the tailgate of the pickup. We were all laughing in disbelief as we boarded and took our seats. My first unpleasant surprise was that I only had half a seat belt. There was no way I could strap in with only half of the strap. After the 29 of us had taken our seats the rest of the occupants of this expected flight began boarding as well. It was too late for me to change seats so I just smiled and shook my head in disbelief. When every seat on the plane was filled I, sitting by a window seat, saw about 30 soldiers complete with rifles marching towards our plane in single file. They began climbing the stair case and I turned around and confirmed there were no more seats available. As they entered the airplane the flight attendant took their rifles and placed them in the closet. The soldiers continued down the aisle towards the rear of the plane. When all 30 soldiers were on board the plane and standing in the aisle from the very back of the plane to the front of the cabin we began our taxi, out to our take off position. We turned on to the runway and the captain pushed the throttles to full power for takeoff. The plane thrust forward and at once my seatback went from the full upright position to a fully reclining position. I was hanging on for dear life to my one half seat belt and the Chinese guy behind me shoved my seat back up to the full upright position once again. The standing soldiers were grasping for better hand holds to the storage racks built near the ceiling and they were all laughing.

Our destination was a one hour flight away and as we sped along I noticed when looking out the window the sky was getting overcast. And the ground was fading out of view but at my last sighting there was still snow on the ground. So far on this trip since we had left Hong Kong we have been too cold to take a bath or shower since there has been no heat in our hotels. If the outside temperature was 20 degrees it is more than likely the indoor temperature was close to that as well. To make things worse if we were in a hotel with American style toilets there was usually a sheet of ice covering the water in the bowl. On top of that (if that isn't bad enough) the pipes were frozen or the water was turned off because we had no water at the faucets in our bathrooms. If we had sit down style American toilets we felt privileged because most of the toilets in China were Chinese style. That style consisted of raised footsteps on the floor where you place your feet and a hole in the center between them. The user assumes the position of a baseball catcher and pray that your aim is still on target. (No curve balls here please)!

Needless to say the entire trip so far was turning out to be a real education for all of us. We had partaken in every kind of food ranging from snake, rat, dog, fish eye soup and chicken head soup with real chicken heads. We ate fish, duck, geese, pork that tasted like fish and beef that tasted like pork. We were on our final decent into Hangzhou and looking out the window I could clearly see it was very foggy. The plane was getting lower and lower and slowing down considerably but I still could not see the ground. Once in a while I could hear and feel the engine accelerate and we were weaving back and forth in an apparent attempt to find the airport. I was getting nervous to say the least and I had a very tight grip on my half seat belt. The soldiers stood there calmly as if this were 'old hat' for them. I looked out the window again just in time to see a radio tower or something looking like a radio tower go whizzing past, not 20 feet off our wing tip. Holy smoke, that was close! Then suddenly the engines idled back and we were on the ground. Thank goodness!!!! The tarmac had been cleaned of snow and when we came to a complete stop the now familiar pickup truck with the fancy stair case pulled up to offload we passengers. The soldiers deplaned first followed by my group and me. As my feet touched the good earth after the giant step from the wood box I turned to look at the plane. It had to be a very old plane as the paint was peeling off the letters CAAC and the aluminum fuselage appeared to be oxidized. Then one look at the tires and I could not believe my eyes. There were two wheels and tires at the end of the landing gear attached to the left wing. Three of those four tires had the canvas showing. The fourth tire had tread showing but very little.

In hind sight I must say that after a while I got used to the sub standard flying conditions in China as I was forced to fly CAAC on many occasions after that first one.

We visited several more cities and my trusting and gracious interpreter was still by my side and still asking questions about America.

Then with five more days to go on this gruelling trip and still not having had the opportunity for a shower we arrived in Beijing, known at that date as Peking. We had spent 17 days in freezing weather and freezing hotel rooms. We had slept in summer resort lodges where it was 15 degrees above zero and slept on straw mattresses. Some of those straw mattresses were covered with linen sheets and some were not. On at least one occasion I shared my straw mattress with some critter that needed my body warmth as well as his own. (a rat). At one of our infamous happy hours, Bruce, our gay friend jumped on top of the bed he was sitting on and began screaming like a little girl. When I jumped up to look at him he was pointing at Harriet. When I looked at Harriet there was the biggest rat I had ever seen under her chair standing on his hind feet with his nose in the air sniffing the sweet odor of the goodies she carried with her in that giant purse. When I went to the door leading to the outside and removed a towel I had previously stuffed under the two inch gap between the floor and the door Harriet asked what I was doing. I was busy wrapping the towel around my hand and arm, with full intentions of punching that rat to his death. At the last moment Harriet said 'don't do it Merrill don't do it'. I reluctantly asked why and she said 'we will probably have to eat him at breakfast'. With that, the entire group burst out laughing. We chased the rat out of the room and returned the towel under the door.

Our last flight, that took us to Beijing, was our last port of call before leaving China. If we had not already filled our brains with new and remarkable memories we learned it was not over yet.

We were driven from the airport to the Beijing Hotel next to Tiananmen Square. It was extremely cold in Beijing and we were not looking forward to more freezing nights under down comforters. Most of the hotels we stayed in China were made of concrete and they all had 10 to 12 foot ceilings

We were pleasantly surprised when we entered the ancient but classic Peking Hotel and found the lobby was warm as toast. Just as soon as I doled out the room keys to the group members we were off to our rooms for a long hot shower!!!! Can you imagine going 17 days without a shower? I soaked for at least 45 minutes and cherished every second of it! My clothing reeked so I called for room service and had my suit and tie sent to the dry cleaners and my socks, undershorts, shirts and hankies sent to the laundry.

After a fresh shave and dressing into fresh clothing I made my way to the lobby bar for a relaxing drink. As I walked to an empty table I noticed what appeared to be four American people sitting at a table nearby. Within a minute that suspicion was confirmed when I heard them speaking perfect English. Both the women were beautiful and one of the gentlemen was vaguely familiar. I ordered a Black Label with water on the rocks and was surprised when they served me that drink. Our personal stock had long since been exhausted. I had no sooner taken my first swig when I was joined by a fresh looking Chung Ching Kuo. He sat down and told me that two American movie stars were staying at our hotel. I asked him who they were and he ran to the front desk to find out. He returned with the news that it was William Holden and Stephanie Powers and two of their friends. Here I was sitting several tables away from them.

Soon my group members came trickling into the bar and when we were all present we left on the bus for a restaurant and a delicious dinner.

At the turn of the century when the Peking Hotel was first built it had to be a sight to behold. The bathrooms were all made of heavy ceramic tile and the huge four footed bath tubs equipped with polished brass exposed plumbing was gorgeous!

My bed had a real mattress (no straw) and with the push of a button on my bed stand I could open and close my drapes covering the gigantic windows. We actually had TV in our rooms but there was only one channel and that was Chinese speaking only.

The following morning we boarded the bus for the long drive up the mountains to view and walk on the Great Wall of China. The Great Wall of China took more than 300 years to complete and it spanned over a 3000 miles. Millions on men died from over work and exhaustion and their blood and bones were used in the mortar but the work continued. The wall itself was twenty five feet high and twenty five feet wide. It had guard stations about every 100 yards and the top of the wall was wide enough for four horseman to ride side by side and patrol the wall. On both sides of the wall the stones were mortared higher than the top of the wall to make a barrier so to speak to keep horses and men from falling off. The wall was built to keep the Manchurians from invading China but unfortunately the wall was not effective in that regard. The failure of the wall to protect China led at least one emperor to commit suicide. Everyone took photos and purchased souvenirs.

Then it was on to see and tour the Ming Tombs. They thought a lot of their former leaders and the mile long road into the tombs was lined on both sides with limestone carved statues of exotic animals. There were lions, tigers, elephants, giraffes, buffalo, unicorns and many more, some not even identifiable. The tombs themselves were dug far into the side of a mountain and hidden by covering the entrance after the emperor was buried. No one knows for sure how many former emperors were buried there and they just call the area the Valley of the Kings. It was again a long day and that night we were treated to a Chinese opera at a beautiful and ornate theatre. It was colorful and spectacular but the music was foreign and a bit boring. The Chinese soldiers were still marching past our hotel at four AM in the mornings as they were in every city we visited. Soldiers were everywhere! Frequently fighter jets would swoop down, close over our heads, scaring the living daylights out of us. When asking Chung the reason for that display his response sent chills up my spine. His reply was "the Chinese government wants to instill in Americans minds that there is no way American fighters can win a war against China".

The second morning in Beijing found us boarding a bus for a short ride to the Forbidden City. This was another awe inspiring adventure and quite educational in a historic view. The forbidden city stretches for miles and it too is surrounded by a high stone wall. It had to be a spectacular experience to be an emperor as he did nothing more than sleep, eat, and satisfy his sexual desires with any one of his eight hundred concubine. His servants were all eunuchs so he had no worries about any other man messing around with any of his girlfriends. There is a story that both China and Japan take credit for and that is this.

You have heard the term "not my cup of tea". As the story goes the emperor, every once in a while wanted to add to his concubine. He would send one or two of his eunuch's outside the forbidden city walls to find the most beautiful young women they could find. Once the eunuch's had a few young girls they were brought back inside the forbidden city and dressed in the finest most revealing clothing that money could buy. The emperor was given a cup of tea as he sat on his throne. One by one the frightened young women were brought in front of the emperor and forced to expose the most private parts of their body to him. So as to not offend the young girl by sending her away if he did not approve of her he simply said the words, 'this is not my cup of tea' and one of his servants would take the cup from his hand and another eunuch would escort the young lady from the forbidden city. It would have been fun to be an emperor for a week or so, don't you think?

Unbeknownst to my group and me, a very startling event occurred at the Peking Hotel that morning after we had left for our tour. Upon our return to the hotel that afternoon we learned that William Holden and his male friend had decided to take a walking tour by themselves that morning. Chinese people were still gathered around the entrance of the hotel to catch a glimpse of foreigners whom they had never before seen. As the two men made their way through the crowd that was gathered there, suddenly a man who obviously did not share the kind and friendly feelings the majority of the Chinese people felt, broke through the crowd with a small pocket knife in his hand. He slashed at the chest of the man that was with William Holden, missing his mark but hitting his upper arm. The blade sliced through his top coat and his sweater but never touched his skin. With military everywhere the man was arrested immediately. He was taken into custody and tried on charges of attempted murder.

The following morning William Holden and his friends departed the Beijing Hotel for the airport and their long flight back to the states.

When my group and I were gathered in the lobby for our trip to the summer palace I was informed by Chung that our presence was required outside the entrance of the hotel to witness Chinese justice. As we exited the hotel there were as usual all the Chinese people there to greet us. In the center of the mass of people were a large group of soldiers. We were escorted through the crowd and found a man with his hands shackled behind his back. He was on his knees and while we stood there watching, one of the military officers read from a book he held. He was reading in a loud voice. When he finished he slammed the book closed and said something to the soldier standing next to him. With no hesitation the soldier took his hand gun from its holster and in one quick movement brought the weapon to the back of the shackled man's head and squeezed the trigger. With a loud "POP" the man convulsed and fell forwards on his face with blood spurting from the back of his head. We could not believe what we had just seen. At the same time one of the military officers came to us and began talking to us in Chinese. George Stoner passed out and his wife was vomiting. The rest of us were standing there numb and frozen in place. We all were white with fear and disbelief. Chung interpreted to me what the military man said. "It was with great pleasure that we the Peoples Republic of China, demonstrated Chinese justice to our new American friends. Be assured that anyone who attempts to harm, in any way, our valued visitors and friends, will be dealt with in a similar fashion". With that we were dismissed and we boarded our bus for the tour of the summer palace.

What an experience. I do not think many of the group remembered much of the tours we took that day.

That afternoon my laundry and dry cleaning was returned to my room with surprising results! My suit and ties as well as my underwear, socks and shirts had been washed, starched, dried and ironed. I was never able to wear that suit again and if you have never worn starched socks and underwear I do not recommend you try that.

Having been to China many times since I can tell you a bit about the summer palace.

One of the most recent emperors replaced the concubine with an empress. The empress loved the water and wanted her summer palace to be lake side. The emperor wanted the summer palace to be close enough to the Forbidden City that travel to the summer palace could be achieved in a one days chariot ride. Unfortunately there were no lakes within the parameter of his requirement but that did not stop the emperor. He ordered more than one million men to begin digging a 40 acre lake at least 6 feet deep with an island and a bridge to the island. The dirt that was removed from the lake bed was to be piled up to make a mountain on one side of the lake. When this was accomplished a palace was built on the side of the manmade mountain to accommodate the emperor and his wife. The empress wanted to have a large boat but was subject to motion sickness so a marble boat was manufactured which was securely seated on the bottom of the lake. It was approximately 70 feet long and 25 feet wide and had pillars all around. There were many rooms inside and you could board the boat because it was built near the shore line and a marble walkway was built for the short walk out to the boat. The Chinese people went to unlimited expense to please their emperor.

Our time in China was drawing to a close and on the 21st day we made our way to the airport for the long flight back to America and all the comforts we enjoy and too often take for granted.

It is my belief that if more Americans would see how people live in other parts of this great earth there would be less crime and without a doubt more appreciative of the many riches we enjoy and take for granted.

CHAPTER 23

Leaving Philippine Airlines

I n 1980 I was faced with a dilemma. Donna and I lived on a boat that was paid for and we had no "write off's" of any kind. She was an executive secretary to the regional manager of Continental Airlines and I was the sales manager of Philippine Airlines. Together our joint incomes put us in a very high tax bracket. The accountant I was using at that time suggested I invest in a business of some kind in order to get some legitimate reduction in our tax burden. When I mentioned the only business I knew anything about was the horse business he suggested I enter into that venture. When I explained that living on a boat is hardly conducive to raising horses he said boarding horses at a boarding farm was deductible. I began thinking of that scenario and the more I thought of it the more I liked the idea.

I went on a search for a few good thoroughbred racing mares that had been retired because of their age and not because of injury. It was a challenging search but about four weeks later I located a 6 year old brood mare named "Jan's Hope". She was a great grand daughter of the famous "Bold

Ruler" a former Kentucky stud with incredible racing statistics! After some rigorous negotiation we came to agreement on a price and I went in search of a horse trailer. A did find a beautiful goose neck 6 horse trailer but I had two more very big draw backs. First, and most importantly, my vehicle was a Cadillac El Dorado Biarritz. Hardly the vehicle to pull a 40 foot gooseneck 6 horse van. So I needed a truck to pull it. I went in search of a truck big enough to pull a trailer of this size comfortably. I settled on a new GMC one ton truck powered with a 454 cu in motor. My last problem was that the trailer was manufactured in Sacramento, California. My truck was painted in two tone, metallic gray and charcoal. Since I was having this trailer made for me I called the manufacturer in Sacramento and asked him to paint the trailer with GMC colors and I gave him the color code numbers so that the trailer would match the truck. Meanwhile I located another brood mare named "B's My Style". She was a grand daughter of the famous Nashua. We agreed on a price and I began my new venture with just two brood mares to see how things work out. I had already spent more money than we had planned on but at least my venture had begun. I finally got the call that my trailer was finished and ready for pickup so off to Sacramento I went to retrieve my new trailer.

It was about the same time that president Marcos of the Philippines was deposed and Philippine Airlines being owned by a gentleman by the name of Benigno Toda decided to sell his airlines to the government of the Philippines. Change was on its way and that change did not look promising for our American sales staff. I decided to resign from Philippine airlines and devote my full time to my horse business.

In my travels over the previous number of years I had found this small village about 26 miles southeast of Seattle called Enumclaw. It was a cute little Swiss style village nestled in the foot hills of Mount Rainier. I decided to look around there for some land to build my thoroughbred horse farm. I did find a 24 acre piece of land with a nice trout stream flowing through it on the south end of the property. I finally did purchase the property at a very good price and contracted a builder to build my horse barn. I designed the barn myself and it would accommodate 14 horses in 10 foot by 12 foot box stalls. It also had a studio apartment for a hired hand as well as a 10 by 12 shower for the horses with hot and cold water. It had a feed room for grain bins as well as a tack room. The loft held 30 tons of hay and straw which could be dropped into the hay bins from above and the straw could be dropped into the box stalls also from above. I designed the 3600 square foot house with my rear deck featuring a spectacular view of Mount Rainier. I had the entire 24 acre property fenced and cross fenced in three rail wood fencing featuring Kentucky black paint throughout. It was my Shangri la! Just prior to completion I was off to Kentucky with my brand new horse trailer and truck to get my two mares bred to a couple "high powered" Kentucky bred stallions which I had already decided on. Jan's Hope was to be bred by a stud named "Grey Legion", a son of Secretariat, standing at Spendthrift Farms in Lexington. "B"s My Style was to be bred to a stud named "In Good Taste", a son of Nashua, standing at West End Farms also in Lexington.

This was a two week ordeal as both mares had to be enticed into heat by teasing with a teaser stallion to "get them in the right mood"!

Finally "Style" showed that she was ready for a stallion and "In Good Taste" was brought to the breeding shed for "his purpose of being there". The following day I was to catch a flight to Seattle to attend a dinner engagement at an awards banquet hosted by Continental Airlines. The following morning I received a phone call at my hotel room from Spendthrift Farms saying that "Hope" was ready for a stallion and I should make myself available should they need to contact me. I immediately called Donna and asked her if I could possibly forego the flight to and from Seattle due to the up coming breeding that was to take place. My wonderful understanding wife said "of course honey, I understand" and that was a decision I made that I will never forgive myself for. "Hope" was bred that afternoon and I was awakened the following morning at around 3 AM by a phone call. It was a friend of mine by the name of Rich Domzalski. As I was shaking the sleep from my brain I heard him saying that Donna had been in an accident and that I should probably get on a plane and fly back to Seattle. It took several minutes for what he was telling me to sink in and when it did my heart stopped! What happened next is covered in the next chapter. Suffice it to say, that phone call changed my life forever.

CHAPTER 24

El Dorado Farms
and tragedy

I n 1981 I resigned my position at Philippine Airlines to devote full time to my lifelong ambition of raising horses. I purchased 24 acres of beautiful lush grassland with the Neuwakum Creek flowing through it. The land was located near Enumclaw, Washington a pretty little town nestled in the foot hills of the Cascade Mountains and at the very foot of Mount Rainier. The high light feature of this property was the view of Mount Rainier. I fell in love with it the first time I laid my eyes on it. In my mind's eye I could picture a comfortable house near the front of the property and a barn with enough room to house a dozen or more brood mares further back. Donna had been getting restless living on a boat for 8 years and I too could stand a change in scenery and life style. The previous year my tax accountant had suggested I needed a "write off" because a very large portion of our combined income (Donna's & mine) was taken by the government in taxes. We had no mortgage or expenses of any real significance. He suggested I buy some horses. When I told him the improbable idea of keeping horses while living on a boat he responded that everything I spent on the keeping of horses would be a "write off", including the boarding out of horses.

So I located a few thoroughbred broodmares that each had fairly good race records at various race tracks on the west coast. One of the mares was a great grand daughter of a very famous horse named Bold Ruler, one of the foundation sires of the thoroughbred industry. Another mare was a granddaughter of another famous sire named "Nashua". Both had race records in "Bold type" and with some research I found what I felt was the perfect sires to breed them too although these sires were both located in Kentucky.

I purchased a 40 foot horse trailer and a truck to pull it with and began building my horse farm. Donna and I chose the name of 'El Dorado Farms' for this new venture and I hired King Construction to build my 14 stall horse barn. This barn was going to be special as I wanted special horses. I designed it to have a place to shower the horses with warm water and drain the water into a holding pond I would dig about 50 yards from the barn. Later when building the house I would have all the water from the down spouts as well as the ground seepage piped down hill and into the holding pond. I also designed a studio apartment in the barn that would serve as an office as well as living quarters for a hired hand should I ever need one. At the same time I hired a saw mill to cut thousands of 4X6 fence posts and 10,000 running feet of 2X6 fence railing to fence and cross fence the entire property.

While this construction was being done I hired a local contractor to build our new home which Donna and I designed as well. It was a daylight basement house and we designed it to have a large deck on the back side of the house with an unmatched view of Mt. Rainier. We built it with four bedrooms and 3 1/2 baths and it covered 3600 square feet of living space. From the time I purchased the property to the time it was completed and livable took just 5 months. We were living our dream!

It wasn't long before I was being approached by race horse owners to take "layup" horses. Lay up horses are horses that are coming off the race track with injuries that need time to heal or horses that are just plain tired of racing and need some time off. I was getting too busy to be able to handle all this work alone so I hired a young girl named Cindy to help out. She was a good worker and with a little guidance she became very good at picking and cleaning stalls as well as other chores that needed to be done around the farm.

Donna continued her position at Continental Airlines and I spent my days running the farm and planning my breeding program.

Gestation for horses takes 11 months and the goal of any breeder is to have a horse bred in time that the foal would be born as close to (but not before) January of the year. That means that any mares that are successfully bred in February of any year would more than likely give birth to a foal in January of the following year. This is the perfect scenario for a race horse because if they are entered in their first race as a two year old you want them to be born as close to the first of the year as possible since horses birthdays are basically all on January first. For example if you had a foal born in May of 1985 and my foal was born in January of 1985, they would both be running as two year olds in the year 1987. My horse would have the advantage because mine is nearly five months older than your horse.

So it was in late January 1982 when I set off for Kentucky and Spendthrift Farms to have one mare (Jan's Hope) bred to a stallion named Gray Legion who is a son of Secretariat. Another mare (B's My Style) was sent to a private farm and was bred to a stallion named "In Good Taste", a son of Nashua. B's My Style stayed right at West End Farms where "In Good Taste" stood at stud, but Jan's Hope had to be boarded at a farm away from the breeding farm because there were horses there from all over the world being bred to some of the stallions and Spendthrift was full up. I rented a hotel room in Lexington for the month I was there waiting for both mares to be settled. (confirmed pregnant). Mares come into heat every 21 days and "Hope" was the first to show signs she was ready.

At 4 o'clock in the morning I was awakened by my ringing telephone. I brushed the cobwebs from my brain as fast as I could and answered the phone. It was my friend Rich calling from Seattle. How weird!!! It's one AM in Seattle! I will never forget his words. Donna has been in an accident Merrill!!! Chills went through me like a lightning strike! I asked "where is she" and he said "Valley General Hospital in Auburn". I asked if it was serious and he said he thought it was. I asked for the hospital phone number and he gave it to me. I was shaking like a leaf and finally got through to the hospital. I told them who I was and that Donna was my wife. They informed me that she was in the emergency room and I asked if I could talk to her. They hesitated for a few moments and said she was not able to speak! I nearly fainted!!!

I could have kicked myself about then because I had planned to fly out to Seattle that morning to join Donna for an awards banquet that her company was hosting that evening. I had called her the day before and told her that "Hope" was "Horsing" (coming in heat) and would she mind going to the banquet without me. Donna was so gracious and I already knew she would say she didn't mind and that is exactly what she said.

The last thing the nurse said to me before I hung up the phone was "you should probably get out here as soon as you can as she is hurt pretty bad". I was sick. I packed my bags as quick as I could and headed for Chicago O'hare Airport. I told the girl behind the counter, this was an emergency, that my wife had been in an accident and I needed to get to Seattle as fast as I could. The flight was to leave in 20 minutes but it seemed like hours. Finally I boarded the flight to Seattle and soon we were airborne and heading nonstop to Seattle. About four hours later we landed in Seattle and some of my friends that had heard about the accident were there to meet me. They drove me to the auburn Hospital. It was now nearly 12 hours since the accident had occurred. I rushed to the front desk and identified myself and asked to see my wife. I was told she was still in surgery!!! My legs went weak and I thought I would fall down. This cannot be happening; this has to be a dream!!! It wasn't! I was escorted to the double swinging doors that led to the operating room and was asked to sit there on one of the chairs and that I could see her as they wheeled her past on the way to ICU.

Finally what seemed like hours later a nurse approached me and said your wife will be coming through those doors in a few minutes. It has now been 14 and 1/2 hours that Donna was in surgery.

Suddenly the double doors swung open and four to five people were around the gurney as it rushed past! Two nurses were carrying bags of liquid over their heads and tubes were going from the bags to her arms and another was "breathing" for her with a large balloon type device they were squeezing. I walked along side and was studying the face on the stretcher and I almost screamed, "this is not my wife"! Whoever was on that stretcher was not my wife and I suddenly had a glimmer of hope that someone had mistaken identity?

I was stopped at the doors of the ICU and told I could not enter until they had the patient set up with IV's etc. I told them it was a mistake that I could clearly see that it was not my wife and they assured me that she had been identified as Donna Rae Rosenberger from her driver's license and credit cards etc.

I stumbled back to a chair and flopped down and began crying like a baby. Soon a nurse came by and told me the head surgeon would be coming out to speak with me shortly. I was in for another shocking experience.

The doors again swung open to the operating room and here came a black man. He walked up to me and asked if I was Mr. Rosenberger. My mind was going nuts! On one side I was thinking 'if she dies or if there is anything at all wrong with her after this ordeal I will personally kill you'! My other thought was 'please tell me she is going to be OK'. He sat down beside me and introduced himself as Doctor Cumberbatch. He placed his hand on my shoulder. His words will forever ring in my ears!

"Mr. Rosenberger, there are a lot of things that could take your wife's life. She has gone through so very much! Her lower mandible (jaw) has been shattered. Her cheek bone is broken! Her left arm is broken at 22 places between her wrist and her shoulder. Her right foot was completely disconnected from the ankle bone and she had massive internal bleeding! All these things are not going to effect the life of your wife. These are just the minor things that she has encountered. The more serious things are that she has ruptured intestines, ruptured liver, a collapsed lung, bruised heart, and even more serious, her pancreas has been divided!!! These are the things that could take your wife's life"!!!! He went on to say that she was given 14 units of blood during the nearly 14 hours of surgery.

I asked the dreaded question "is she going to live"??? He answered "she does not have a very good chance". I began crying again and he held me for a minute.

He asked if I believed in prayer and I said yes! He said let's see what the next 24 hours brings. If she can make it until this time tomorrow it will be the first step. He then said if she does make it until tomorrow do not get your hopes up because the worse is yet to come. I asked, 'how can that be' and he said because her bruised heart may not be able to withstand the damage that has been done and the pancreas could explode upon itself at any time. By this time I was becoming numb to all the information I was given and my mind ceased functioning. He explained that the acid in the pancreas is so powerful that you cannot stitch it, not even with stainless steel stitches! He went on to say that the only choice he had was to bury the two halves of the pancreas inside the intestine which is the only part of the human body that can withstand that acid. He explained that it is a procedure called a Roux en Roi (obviously a French discovery).

Hours passed and finally I was allowed to see Donna. As I approached the bed I could see that she was not conscious and she was on a respirator. Her face was swollen and distorted and I could see stitches that went from the corner of her mouth clear back to her right ear. Donna was in a coma. It took my imagination to accept the fact that the body I was looking at did in fact belong to my wife. I touched her right hand and it was cold. Her color was pale and I could hear the machine as it was breathing for her through a hole they had cut in her neck. My poor Donna! How I wished this had happened to me and not to her. I was told she had never lost consciousness throughout time of the accident and the extraction from the car and the ambulance ride to the hospital. My God, how did she stay conscious through this!!!

Orders came down from the head surgeon that visitors would be limited to immediate family members only. I was the only immediate family member in the area as her family was all located in Texas. My family was located back in Pennsylvania.

It angered me to the point of insanity, the following day I learned that one of Donna's colleagues (Dave Wharf) had arrived at the hospital after I had left to take a badly needed shower at a friends house. Learning that visitors were limited to immediate family, Mr. Wharf told the ICU nurse that he was her husband! This new nurse had not met me and knew no better and allowed this stupid curiosity seeker to enter the ICU and to this day I resent him for his total lack of respect not to me but to Donna!

Donna remained in a coma for another week and I was living at the hospital, leaving just long enough each day to shower and shave. About the 8th day Donna finally opened her eyes when I touched her hand as I always did when visiting her. I would talk to her even knowing she could not respond and not even knowing for sure she was hearing me. I would beg her to keep fighting and not to give up that she would be fine. Unable to speak because of the tracheotomy Donna indicated with hand motions she wanted to write something. I excitedly asked the nurse for some writing material and a pen. She gave me a tablet and pen and I held the tablet while Donna wrote the following: 'this hotel is so very noisy, can we go to a different hotel'? Not knowing how to respond to the question I said we will soon and she attempted to get out of bed!!! I screamed 'no Honey'! And she settled back into a reclined position again. She had a huge cast on her right leg that went from her toes up to her hip. Her left arm was in a cast from her fingertips to her shoulder. I could not show her the emotions I was feeling every time I looked at her. She would write "Honey, I love you" and I would tell her I loved her too. She was getting heavy doses of "demoral", morphine and other pain medications on a 24 hour basis. Weeks passed before Dr. Cumberbatch finally came to me and said I can now say that Donna is out of the woods. What a relief. One day Donna wrote 'I wish we could make love' and she looked at me as though I was going to fulfill her desire and all I could say was 'so do I honey, so do I', and I would have to look away from her to hide my disappointment.

Weeks passed and I became a regular fixture in the ICU but she would not be released from that unit for more than a month. When she was, she was placed in a step down unit which was a private room with 24 hour nursing staff present at all times. Dr Cumberbatch placed a hand written message on the door that said "absolutely no visitors". Donna's life was still on a fragile pinnacle and Dr. Cumberbatch told me the message on the door was not intended for me.

He then asked if he could speak to me in private and I agreed of course. We went into the chapel for privacy and sat down. It was then he told me that he had not expected Donna to survive and on a scale of 1 to 10 he had given her a minus 3 chance! He told me that he actually believed the reason for her recovery was because of my steadfast attendance by her side throughout the entire ordeal and the love we had for each other.

Donna and I were still communicating, with Donna writing notes and me answering verbally. How I wanted to hear her sweet voice. A chest tube had been inserted in her side, under her right arm, to inflate her collapsed lung before she even had gone into surgery the night of the accident. That tube was still there. The tracheotomy was still in her neck that enabled her to breath. It was with great excitement I felt, when the doctor told me that he would be removing the chest tube and tracheotomy in a few days. What wonderful news!!! He reminded me that this would be an experimental procedure only because if she was not able to breath on her own she would be put back on the respirator. I prayed like I had never prayed before and several days later Dr. Cumberbatch came in with two nurses to withdraw the chest tube and respirator. I watched as Dr. Cumberbatch took a large adhesive patch in his left hand and a firm grip of the chest tube in his right hand. In one swift motion he pulled the tube out and slapped the adhesive patch over the hole that was left from the tube. Donna's face winced as he did this and I am sure it must have hurt. He then reached up to her neck and removed the tube leading to the tracheotomy. I watched to see Donna's reaction. There was none. So far so good! He looked at me and explained that he would leave the tracheotomy in her neck and all she need to do to talk was to put her finger over the hole in the plastic device and she could talk. Donna had not taken anything by mouth for over two months at this time as she had been fed intravenously since her arrival at the hospital. The last thing the Doctor did before leaving us alone in the room was to place the oxygen tube around her ears and the two little nozzles into her nostrils so she could continue getting oxygen without the respirator. When we were finally alone Donna reached up and placed a finger over the hole in the plastic device in her neck and said "I love you Honey"!!! I nearly cried with joy! We hugged and kissed for the first time in two months.

What occurred next was another educational experience for me as it was now time for her to take nourishment by mouth. A different doctor came in for this procedure. He explained that since her intestines had been laid out on the operating room table during surgery and stuffed back in when the surgery was completed there had to be a "test run" to see if her digestion system would allow nourishment to pass through without obstruction. Amazing! The doctor asked her what she would like to drink as the first food would have to be liquid. She chose tomato juice and so it was. She was given a small glass of tomato juice which she drank down. I cannot imagine going for two months without eating or drinking a thing and then drinking a glass of tomato juice. What a taste surprise that must have been for her. The nurses were checking Donna's blood gases regularly to assure she was getting enough oxygen. So far so good!!! One day Doctor Russo came by to say it was time to take the casts off her arm and her leg. He bought a power saw and a nurse and he slowly and carefully began cutting the plaster cast with this circular saw. For the first time I saw the scars on her leg from the accident as well as the surgery that was performed to repair the damage. I saw the scars on her forearm and upper arm from the surgerys at that location as well. She bore a scar from the corner of her mouth to her right ear and her bottom front teeth had been knocked completely out. Although she had been wearing her seatbelt when the car that had struck her head on (drunk driver) had hit her, the steering wheel was pushed back along with the motor and the entire front end of the car. It was the steering wheel that her face hit crushing her lower mandible, tearing her cheek back to her ear. It was also the steering column that pushed into her abdomen, doing all the internal damage to her liver intestines and pancreas as well as her lungs and heart. Donna had 7 doctors including a plastic surgeon as well as a Psychiatrist and several weeks later they all got together for a private meeting with me. They started off by asking me if I had any questions. I asked the plastic surgeon why he hadn't done a better job with the scar on Donna's cheek? His answer stunned me! He said 'if the patient is not expected to live there is no reason to spend tons of money for cosmetic purposes'. He had a smirk on his face and I could have punched him hard right in that smirk! (I was told later by Dr. Cumberbatch that plastic surgeons have habitually a vain and proud attitude and I should not allow that to irritate me). His explanation never did satisfy me.

One by one all the doctors were giving me their final report on Donna's condition before releasing her from the hospital. The arrogant plastic surgeon left the room and the psychiatrist was the last to speak. He was very slow and methodical as he told me that I could expect Donna to be a completely different person than she was before. He explained that a person could not possibly go through the trauma she had experienced and remain the same mentally. I tried to convince him that nothing would change between Donna and I because we were not just husband and wife but we were best friends as well. He stubbornly stayed his theory and that theory was re-affirmed by all the doctors present. I did not believe it and was determined to prove them all wrong.

Two more weeks went by and the plastic device was removed from Donna's neck and the site was stitched closed. Her food was successfully passing through her and I couldn't help but think the comparison had to simulate to starting an engine after a major overhaul. Donna was still in the step down unit when the nurses arrived with a wheel chair and asked if she was ready to go home. That morning I had hired a beautician to give Donna a complete facial and make up including her hair styled. It had been hinted to me the day before that I might want to do that to give Donna a positive attitude. Little did I know then she would be released from the hospital after 3 months of residence.

I was thrilled to the bone!!! Donna took it in stride which surprised me somewhat. I brought the borrowed car I was using around to the front entrance in time to see the nurses and a few doctors wheeling her out the front doors and towards my vehicle. Everyone but Donna was smiling from ear to ear including Dr. Cumberbatch. I walked to his side and hugged him and thanked him for saving the life of my wife. I told him that he would be receiving a token of my appreciation soon. (later I presented him with a solid gold pocket watch and chain with the words "THANK YOU" inscribed on the back.

We drove home to El Dorado Farms in silence as Donna seemed depressed. She was still taking a drug called

Methadrone which is a drug that gets drug addict's off heroine and cocaine. Donna had been on pain medication for so long it was felt necessary to keep her on this drug for a period of time to allow her to retrieve from the pain meds that she had been getting for the past few months. When we arrived home Donna was able to walk on her own although weakened and she sat in the living room as I turned on the TV for her. I waited on her hand and foot but she said nothing.

Going to bed that evening was another disappointment for me as after three long months Donna did not feel like being affectionate. That hurt me to the core but I used the excuse that she was still recovering. I went about my daily chores and Cindy had kept the farm running perfectly for the time I was gone although I did check in with her daily via telephone. My truck was still sitting in the parking lot at the Chicago O'hare airport. I asked one of Donna's best friends if she would be kind enough to stay with Donna at the farm while I flew back and retrieved my truck, trailer and of course my now very pregnant mares. I then called a good friend of mine a Mr. Joseph Bays, a King County Police officer to ask if he would be able to accompany me to Kentucky to assist in the long drive back to El Dorado Farms. He agreed and the following day we flew back to Chicago, retrieved my truck and began the drive south to Lexington KY.

I paid my bills, loaded my very pregnant horses and Joe and I started the long trip back to El Dorado Farms. I had a sleeping birth in the front section of the trailer and we drove 24 hours a day switching off and on getting sleep when we could. I had a telephone from the cab of the truck to the sleeper in the trailer and we could communicate if we needed to simply by pressing the call button. We arrived back at El Dorado three and a half days later. I had paid for all of Joe's expenses and he refused any payment I offered for his help. What a friend!!! When I entered the house Donna was sitting in the same chair she had been sitting in when I left. Instead of the familiar jumping up and running into my open arms she sat and waited as I walked over and kissed her. She turned her head and I kissed her on the cheek and my heart was sinking slowly. The pain increased daily as she continued her cold, but still polite treatment towards me and after a few months she finally said the words I dreaded to hear but felt they were coming. She had stopped calling me "sweetie", "honey", "darling" and other affectionate names since arriving home from the hospital. She was now calling me Merrill if anything at all. This time she called me into the living room to announce that she had contacted an attorney and was filing for a divorce. The feeling I got from that statement was very similar to the feeling I had when I first learned she had been in an accident. I knew that things were no longer the way they were before the accident but now I had to prepare for even worse. That night for the first time she moved into and slept in the guest bedroom. It broke my heart. The following morning I tried to speak to her by asking why and what can I do? Her answer was cold and determined and she said life is too short and I need to be alone. The next time I asked if there was something I could do to change her mind she said we were not growing together. It was useless and I knew it. Try as I might I could not break through that hard cold shell she had built around herself. The day came and I was served with divorce papers and Donna moved away to an apartment near Des Moines, a small town south of Seattle, but close to the airport where she was still employed. I gave her the Cadillac and kept the truck for myself. My dream farm would never be the same. As much as I hated the thought of selling my dream property I knew I would never be happy there without Donna so I reluctantly called a local realtor and listed El Dorado for sale. It was a post card view farm and how I hated what I was doing, but it had to be done.

One by one I sent the boarding horses elsewhere for places to stay for layover and several months later a serious buyer made an offer which offered a modest profit for my investment. I had no choice but to accept this offer and with a broken heart I walked away from my dream.

Ironically it was just before I left the property of El Dorado that I received a call from Tyler Tanaka the owner of a land operation company in Los Angeles, CA. I had known him throughout my employment with Philippine Airlines and had worked with him on a regular basis in those years. He wanted to know if I would be interested in being a tour director to destinations in the Orient and South East Asia. Suddenly I thought of the slogan that says when God closes one door He always opens another. This opportunity was not to be ignored as it is quite possible that this is what I need to get my mind off the devastating losses I just suffered. I knew the Orient and South East Asia like the back of my hand so I jumped at the opportunity and accepted the offer. A week later I had moved my remaining furniture into a duplex in Enumclaw and was on a flight to Los Angeles to meet with Mr. Tanaka. He did not waste any time as I filled out the proper papers and agreed to the conditions of the contract which I signed.

It was October of 1983 and as I flew back to Seattle I was already planning my first trip to Japan and the Orient that was leaving in four days hence! That is another chapter!

CHAPTER 25

Familiarization Trips

M y very first trip as a tour director was not a group of tourists but a group of travel agents on a familiarization trip. The purpose of these trips was to educate travel agents to the destinations they send their clients to on a regular basis. It is not a vacation and it should be considered a working trip. I was not only now contracted to Japan and Orient tours, I was also sub contracted to United Airlines who provided the free flight for this group of agents in both directions across the Pacific Ocean. We generally visited three or more countries on these orientation trips. I was given strict rules and regulations by United Airlines because they were giving away as many as 25 seats worth $1500.00 each for these trips. They expected a return on their investments by these agents learning the destinations and promoting them to their clients. I had a strict itinerary, conducted more like a business college than a tour of sightseeing tourists.

In Japan for instance I would take a group of 25 travel agents and break them into 5 separate groups of five, upon arrival in Tokyo. I would assign one person as the group leader, one would be the navigator and one would be the treasurer. The remaining two were the reporters that would give me the report on all the questions I was to ask upon the conclusion of their assignment. I would send each group to a different precinct of Tokyo. One group would tour Maranuchi, one group would tour Ginza, and one group would tour Akasaka and so forth. The navigator would decide how the group would travel to their area either by taxi, subway, bus or walking. Each group was given a map and had to figure these things out for themselves with no help from me. The treasurer had to keep track of the cost of the travel expenses incurred throughout their individual means of travel.

At the end of the day when the groups all returned to our hotel there would be a meeting in my suite to discuss what had been learned by each and every group. Although each group had the experience of their specifically assigned area the entire group would benefit from the report that was given of each of the different precincts. After the first day I would take the group on a tour of my own design showing them the more popular places to send their clients such as the fish market at 4 o'clock in the morning or a particularly beautiful shrine or water falls etc. I had to direct these tours with a strong authority because travel agents getting a free ride and free meals tend to think they are on vacation. I was given authority by United Airlines to send anyone home ahead of time if they refused to accept their responsibility of taking these mandatory educational tours. (I only had to exercise that option once).

These tours usually lasted for a maximum of 7 days for a one or two country tour and no longer than 10 days for a three country tour.

There was no real good money to be made when escorting travel agents but the purpose of giving me experience in directing a tour was one of the advantages and I learned my lessons well. For example I learned early on it is more important for a tour director to be a dictator that a democracy. I learned this one day when I decided to ask the group of agents if they would rather go to Nara Japan to see the largest Buddha in the world inside a building or to take a beautiful cruise on a large pristine lake. The group was split, half wanting to go to one place, the other half wanting to go the other place. That was impossible and I made an executive decision and angered half the group! Lesson learned! I am glad I made that mistake with travel agents and not paying tourists.

After several more travel agent groups I was finally given my first group of paying customers! What a pleasant experience that was compared to travel agents who were always complaining about the cost of meals or having to pay for a taxi to get somewhere. I was originally tempted to title a book on travel agents with the words "What Do You Mean it ain't Free"! I chose not to, after careful consideration.

To be a successful tour director one must wear a multitude of hats. Responsibilities range from being a marriage counselor, an adult baby sitter, a psychiatrist a disciplinarian, and a walking, talking dictionary a banking executive, a common laborer and above all a diplomat.

My groups of tourists never had to touch their baggage, if the group size did not exceed 40 people. When arriving at foreign destinations I would ask several of the men to bring a four wheeled cart and follow me with mine as I made our way to the carousel to collect the baggage. Each member of the group was given a color coded heavy cardboard tickets that were to be attached to each and every checked bag. I would collect every bag I saw with that color coded tag coming around on the carrousel and stack it on the carts. I had already collected all the passports and airline tickets which were safely stowed in my brief case. I would approach the customs agent at entry and declare the number of members in my group and produce their passports. They were each stamped for entry and given back to me and we proceeded to the waiting bus for our drive to the hotel. I could enter a country as quickly with 40 people or more as fast as I could alone and no one had to handle their baggage as I did it all for them.

The same practice was applied on our exit from a country. There are departure taxes applied to each and every passenger departing any country and it must be paid in cash on departure. The prices varied depending on the country and I collected these monies from the group prior to leaving the hotel for the airport on the day of departure. I would approach the check in counter and pay the departure tax and produce the airline tickets and passports. The passports would be stamped as departing the country and in less than ten minutes we were ready to board our flight for our next destination. It worked like clockwork every time in every country.

Paying tourists have one thing in mind that travel agents never think about when entering a foreign country. That is of purchasing items from the country they are visiting. Example: Hong Kong is Famous for bargains in clothing both men's and women's, Jewelry, eel skin items, cashmere items, watches and electronics as well as furs. As a rule, I as a tour director would receive a whopping 20% commission on every penny that was spent in each and every city visited. In Hong Kong there are many retail tailors. Some were good, some were fair and somewhere no good at all. More than that there are a few that are very good! This was true not just with the custom tailor shops but also the jewelry stores and all the others as well. I had an advantage in that over the years of traveling there with Philippine Airlines I learned quickly who were the very best in the city. As a rule the average a person would spend at the jewelry store was $1000.00. The same for the Tailor shop, another $1000.00!!!

In Thailand for instance the thing people were looking to purchase was Burmese Jade. The average spent was $1000.00 per person. Groups of 40 with that kind of commission, well, you do the math. 20 % on everything that was purchased and it was always paid in U.S. Dollars cash, very discretely in an envelope after dark in the privacy of my hotel suite. My groups were usually of three weeks duration and I would do as many as five or six groups back to back before taking a week or two off for a little R&R. Than it was the flight back across the Pacific for another round of tours with new groups of interesting people.

I must confess that one of the most enjoyable groups I ever directed was a group of 18 very beautiful young women. They were all prior centerfold women from Hugh Hefners Playboy magazine. That trip spoiled me for a very long time as I was pampered the entire way. It was incredible what being surrounded and pampered by so many beautiful women will do to one's ego and it took me a long time to get over it. Just as that was the very best of the hundreds upon hundreds of tours that I took the very worst was a group of Russian citizens.

That's another chapter.

CHAPTER 26

My most difficult group
of tourists ever

In 1989 I was asked to take a group of Russian tourists
on a five country tour. We were to visit Japan, Thailand,
Singapore, Malaysia and Hong Kong. They all were green
card holders living in America and they all spoke English,
although a bit broken.

The tour began without incident but it took a lot of
explaining that they must attach their color coded baggage
I.D. Cards to each and every checked bag. Each passenger was
issued two, color coded I.D. Cards with the name of "Japan
and Orient Tours" printed boldly on one side. It was my aid
to identify my group's baggage when retrieving them from the
carrousel in the baggage claim area. On this particular group
there were 92 checked bags when the group left the USA for this
tour. There were 46 persons in this group. The first problem
arose when we were in flight from Japan to Bangkok, Thailand.
I had gotten out of my seat to stretch my legs when I noticed
one of my passengers was asleep on a pillow resting his head

near the window of the aircraft. I could clearly see the logo of the Akasaka Prince Hotel on the pillow and knew at a glance that it had been stolen from the hotel on our departure. I felt my blood beginning to boil as I could not allow my group members to be stealing from the hotels that I frequent on a regular basis with my different groups of travelers. I said nothing until we were checked in at the Royal Orchid Hotel in Bangkok. I went to the room of the offender and knocked on the door. I was greeted by the husband and told him the purpose of my visit. He did not seem embarrassed in the slightest way at what I just accused him of but replied he liked the pillow so he took it! He then told me that he was not the only one that took things from the hotel. He named another member of the group who had taken a king sized blanket from the bed, in his room of the hotel. I was really upset by this time and decided to make an announcement on our next bus tour. Little did I know that what I had discovered was just the tip of the iceberg.

After several days in Bangkok we again arrived at the international airport for our flight to Singapore. As with all countries, I counted 92 baggage pieces on check in and paid all departure taxes and we boarded our flight to Singapore. When we arrived in Singapore we routinely met in the baggage claim area and I began the chore of collecting all 92 checked bags. Since we travel as a group and check in at the same time our baggage comes off the plane, generally speaking all together. As a result, for some time I am as busy as a "one armed paper hanger" yanking baggage from the carrousel and stacking them on the four wheeled carts. Once they are all on the carts I begin my count and this time I came up with just 91 pieces of luggage! I recounted and again came up with 91 bags. One bag was missing. After one final recount I asked the group members to take a look to see who was missing a piece of luggage. They all looked and all said they had nothing missing. This did not make sense to me because I clearly had 92 bags from the beginning of the tour! I had counted 92 bags at departure from Bangkok so there had to be 92 bags on arrival in Singapore. Again no one said they were missing a bag.

At that point I said "well, I guess we will just sit here until the 92nd bag shows up so you all should just make yourself comfortable". I grabbed my bag and used it as a stool and sat down on it. At that point one of the men came forward and he produced a small bag that he had removed the green color coded tag from and said this is probably the bag you're looking for because I decided I would hand carry it from now on. I could have smacked his face! He had delayed the group for nearly 45 minutes and we were lucky that our local people had not left the airport with the waiting bus ride to our hotel.

After two days in Singapore we were off on a bus ride from Singapore to the country of Malaysia. Several hours later we arrived at our hotel and checked in, followed by a wonderful dinner at a local restaurant, before retiring for the day.

The following morning we took a bus tour of the countryside stopping at a pewter factory for some shopping. In southeast Asia when buying sets of dinner ware you buy in uneven numbers, such as 5, 7, 9, etc. One member of my group decided he wanted a service of six and not of five so when the store clerk was not looking he snatched a 6th pewter setting and stuffed it in his pocket.

Later we were back in the bus heading for our hotel after a long day when I overheard this husband telling the couple sitting in the row in front of him how he had stolen a sixth pewter setting from the pewter store. That did it! I was livid. Without saying a word I walked up to the bus driver and told him to go back to the pewter factory. He found a place to turn the big bus around and back to the pewter factory we went. My own personal reputation was at stake because I go to that pewter store on most visits to Malaysia. When we arrived at the pewter store I went to the unsuspecting thief took him by the arm and marched him inside. Once there in front of the clerk I gave him a choice. Either pay cash for the sixth place setting or return the stolen items. This time the man did show embarrassment!

I made a vow to never guide another Russian group of tourists again.

CHAPTER 27

Chung Ching Kuo and Jack Thompson

In 1979 I had used an interpreter in communist China by the name of Chung Ching Kuo. I had used him on several previous trips and he was a very likeable person. He was extremely curious about the United States and had a million questions. He would ask some like this: "Is it true that parents spank their children in the USA"? "Is it true that all Americans have swimming pools on their property"? "Is it true that all married couples have two cars"?

He carried a notebook and made notes of all he learned and we introduced him to "American slang". On particularly rough roads we called them "washboard avenues" and of course he wrote that down in his note book.

He was extremely aware that we were being spied on by the Chinese government as our rooms were "bugged" and we learned not to say anything negative about the Chinese people or government when we were in our rooms and especially at happy hour.

I believe it was my third trip using Chung as my interpreter when we arrived at the Beijing Hotel in Beijing. Before we disembarked from our bus to retire to our rooms before dinner he informed me he needed to speak to me in private. I automatically assumed I had made a gross error in protocol and was about to be chastised for it so I invited him to my room. As soon as he entered he went right to the TV (in 1979 the Beijing Hotel was the only Hotel in China with television).

He turned the volume up as high as it would go and motioned me to sit on the floor in the center of the room. I no longer thought I had made an error in protocol. What he told me sent chills up my spine!

Earlier that day we had visited a "Friendship Store" in Beijing and these stores were designed for tourists. Every major city had one of these stores but Beijing had the largest one. This was China's version of Macey's accept the Chinese people could never afford to go there in those days. The first floor was typical fancy house coats and smoking jackets with colorful dragons embroidered on them and other things like musical instruments. Handmade violins could be purchased for about $4.00. These violins were not toys, they were real professional. The second floor had housewares and souvenirs and the third floor had furniture. I was intrigued by a particular mahogany bar. It had shelves for the bottles of booze as well as cupboards for glassware and wine glasses. It was plumbed for a wet bar and it was about 5 1/2 feet high and about 6 feet wide and about 2 feet deep. I could have bought it for roughly $90.00 and they would have crated it for shipment. Chung saw me pondering over this piece of furniture and although I was still living on a boat Donna was hinting that we might start looking for some land to build a house or one that was already built.

We were now sitting in the middle of the floor in the living room of my suite with the TV blaring away at full volume.

Chung leaned towards my ear and screamed the words "I want to defect to America"! I nearly choked on my tongue! I leaned towards his ear and said 'let's take a walk outside'. I was sure the blaring TV was going to attract more attention than we needed when having a conversation on a subject such as this! We were watched by official "watchers" but as long as we did not drift to far from the hotel we would not be approached by them. As we walked Chung laid out his plan of escape.

He suggested that I go ahead and purchase the bar I was admiring at the friendship store and have it delivered to my room in the crate ready for shipment. I would then take the lid off the crate and dismantle the bar piece by piece, hiding the wooden pieces in my clothing and taking them out behind the hotel depositing them into a trash container. When the crate was empty Chung would climb inside and I would replace the lid. He said he would take a block of cheese and a thermos of water to drink and he said I would open the crate once we landed in the USA. Before I rejected the idea I asked him why cheese? He said it would make him constipated and the water would keep him from dehydrating. He had obviously thought this plan through fairly well but he under estimated the danger in such an endeavor. It did not take me long to stop him in his tracks and look for other methods of escape. I reminded him that if he was caught during an escape the way he had planned, that we would both suffer death by the Chinese government and I was not willing to pay that price. He agreed but went on to say that he would commit suicide if he could not escape. Having already seen that Chinese men are willing to die rather than live in the condition of their precarious living standards I didn't doubt he meant what he said. I had three more days in China before flying out to Hong Kong so I asked him to allow me to think of a different way. He agreed.

I didn't sleep well that night tossing and turning with Chung's escape on my mind. By the time I went to breakfast I was no closer to a viable plan than I was the day before so I told Chung we would have to write back and forth and if I came up with a plan I would write and tell him. He already had my state side address but I didn't have his. Without hesitation he said "that can't happen either because the Chinese government reads all incoming mail addressed to Chinese people.

I hated the idea that I had gotten so close to Chung that now I was in a very dangerous position. I saw no way out! The day I left for Hong Kong we sat side by side on the way to the Beijing airport. He asked me if I would take a photo of him against a white back ground once we got to the airport and I agreed but asked why. He said he was going to try to get a fake passport made. He then asked me to think up a good American name. I thought he was going to try to give himself an American name but to my surprise he said that would be my name. He went on to explain that I should write my instructions on his escape in a letter and address it to that name at the Beijing Hotel. I came up with the name of Jack Thompson. Since there would be no Jack Thompson staying at the Beijing Hotel, the hotel staff would automatically assume that he would be checking in several days later or so. All mail addressed to anyone not yet checked in at the hotel, was put in an open box and that box was sitting on the counter of the front desk. Chung, residing in Beijing would have the opportunity on a daily basis to flip through that box and when he saw an envelope addressed to Jack Thompson he would pocket it and get his instructions from that letter. The letter would be written in code and was outlined as a strict business letter.

Here is the contents of my first letter to Jack Thompson.

Dear Jack,

Having just finished with my first consulting endeavor in Singapore I am pleased to inform you that my Singaporean colleagues are looking forward for the first shipment from China. I do not foresee any problems with freight being moved to and from China and even the possibility of some freight making its way to the west coast of United States.

This is the way I communicated with Chung when I wasn't in China and speaking to him face to face. When he wanted to communicate with me he simply wrote me a letter and sealed it in an addressed envelope and he would hand it to a trusted tourist to mail for him when they returned to the states or at least when they were out of China. This went on for almost three years.

Then in 1982 I took a month off from my travels and invited my parents to visit Donna and I at El Dorado Farms. It was summer and my dad especially enjoyed driving my Massey Ferguson diesel tractor to the back of my property to the Newakum creek to see the huge salmon that were in that stream spawning. Cindy, my hired hand would sometimes take a pitch fork from the stables and walk down to the stream and throw a salmon on the ground with the pitch fork and take it back to her apartment in the barn and cook it up for dinner. I told her I would not bail her out of jail if she got caught but she never did.

About the third day of my parents visit we were relaxing after having a big lunch and my phone rang. Donna answered it and said it was for me. When I held the receiver to my ear I could tell it was a long distance call and the voice on the other end identified himself as Ian Haley calling from Sydney, Australia. I knew no one from Australia so I just listened as he spoke. He asked if I was Mr Merrill Rosenberger and I said yes. He said I have someone here that wants to speak to you. With that he handed the phone to the unknown caller. The moment I heard the word "Mellow" I knew it was Chung! The Chinese have a difficult time pronouncing their "R's" and "L's" and the closest way they pronounce my name is "Mellow". (some are worse than that)!!!

I was shocked! I asked how he got to Australia and he advised that he was an interpreter and treasurer for a delegation of Chinese dignitaries that were visiting Australia for purposes of filming their wildlife and promoting tourism. He went on to say that he was defecting and has taken the money from the treasury and gone to the home of Ian Haley a tourist he met when he was visiting Beijing. The police had somehow located him and he was going to be put on a plane heading for China in three days and if I could not intercede for him he was going to be executed upon arrival in Beijing! I was stunned! I had long ago decided there was nothing I could do to help my friend escape china and suddenly I was faced with a potential execution that would clearly rest on my shoulders if I couldn't do something to help him. I spoke with Mr. Haley reminding him that Australia was a huge country and could he find somewhere in the outback to hide Chung until this whole ordeal was forgotten. He told me his house was surrounded by Australian authorities and there was no way to get Chung out without detection. I felt like a caged tiger. Panic began to close in on me. I spoke to Chung one more time and told him to keep his head up and I was going to try my best to get him asylum, somewhere. I immediately phoned the White House in an attempt to speak to the president of the United States. It didn't take long for me to realize this was not going to happen. My next step was a call to Scoop Jackson the democratic senator from Washington State. He had just returned from China and would surely understand the urgency of this situation. My first attempt was unsuccessful but on my next call to his Washington DC phone I was told he was at home in Everett, Washington and could be reached at his office phone there. I called the number she gave me and spoke at length with Mr. Jackson about my friend Chung's dilemma. Mr. Jackson totally understood the seriousness of the situation and the inevitable outcome if my efforts were unsuccessful. His reply left me numb from my head to my toes! He explained that America could not go into a foreign country and 'take' a human being from that country and bring him to safety in the USA. He compared that exercise as someone entering another person's home and removing a piece of furniture without the owner's permission. My heart sank as we ended the phone call and I was distraught like never before in my life. I must have sat there looking out the window for more than an hour when I suddenly got an idea! There is an organization called Amnesty International and I desperately went through the phone book looking for a phone number. Finally I called information and was given a number which the phone company connected me to. I explained the entire story to them which must have taken nearly an hour and all they would say was 'we will check into this' I screamed at them there was no time to think that the clock was ticking and there were less than 40 hours left before he was to be taken by the authorities to the Sydney International Airport and flown back to Beijing China and Chung's inevitable death. They hung up on me. 48 hours later I received another phone call from Ian Haley in Sydney saying the police had taken Chung away crying and struggling to get free and he was now on his way to Beijing. All I could do was pray that he didn't suffer and the Chinese would end his life quickly and without pain. I was sick.

A week went by and I still could not free my mind of the terrible thought of my friend Chung's death. Two weeks went by and I was getting no relief from the nightmarish thoughts and dreams. I was losing sleep and felt guilty that I was unable to help my good friend Chung.

Then on a Thursday afternoon about 3:00 PM I received a phone call. Donna was not home and I had been sitting by the window looking outside. I answered the phone and I heard a screaming man yelling MELLO! MELLO I AM FREE I AM FREE!!! Oh my God! Was this true or was I dreaming! I yelled back CHUNG IS THAT YOU? He said YES IT'S ME AND I'M FREE IN TAIWAN!

It took nearly an hour for Chung to fill me in on the events that transpired from the time the police took him from the home of Ian Haley to the airport. He boarded the flight in handcuffs and escorted by two police officers. During the flight they sat on both sides of him and one of them escorted him to the bathroom during the flight. He remained shackled throughout the flight and the plane made a scheduled landing in Hong Kong for re-fueling. As the plane taxied on the tarmac a black limousine came racing out as the big jet came to a stop short of the gate. Two officers boarded the flight removed the shackles from Chung's wrists and ankles and removed him from the aircraft. He was taken to the black limo and sped across the tarmac to another waiting jet owned by China Air, a Taiwanese airplane and a free country. Amnesty International had come through at the last minute. Even then Chung was not free. He was flown to Taipei where he was taken to prison and interrogated for almost two weeks. They suspected that mainland China (Beijing) had sent him as spy and this defection was a scam planned to get him into Taiwan. They tried to break him by keeping him awake for three days running interrogating him relentlessly. They kept asking him who is this Merrill Rosenberger that you keep asking to call on the phone. Finally after nearly two weeks of the same questions over and over Chung said he finally lost his temper and screamed at them if they say one more bad word about my American friend Merrill Rosenberger I was going to punch somebody in the mouth. He said that was the turning point. They sent in a new team of nice interrogators and they were actually paying for the phone call he was making to me.

The end of the story is that Chung Ching Kuo is now a citizen in good standing of the country of Taiwan and is now happily married with children of his own. Sadly I must say that over the years I have lost contact with Chung but I sleep well now that I know he is free. It would be nice to hear the words MELLO MELLO I'M IN AMERICA but I doubt I will ever hear them.

CHAPTER 28

China, the early days

China was a wonderful place to visit back in the late 70's. Not that it is not a great place today, but it was so wild and totally innocent in those days. You could not purchase American products then and if you ran out of your American cigarettes you had two surprises! One was a nice surprise but the other was terrible. In those days a pack of American cigarettes cost around a dollar. On the other hand a pack of 20 cigarettes in China (Chinese tobacco) cost about .12 cents a pack, US equivalent! The taste, however of those cigarettes from China left a lot to be desired. Possibly if you rolled up the dirtiest pair of underwear you ever saw, rolled it in paper and lit the end it just might give you the idea of what I am talking about. A half-gallon of Chivas Regal whiskey in the USA cost around $30.00 but a half-gallon of Chinese Mao Tai was about $3.50 US equivilent. When you first open the bottle of Mao Tai anyone within talking distance would immediately inquire as to what smells of dirty socks! Ah, the good old days! You could buy a professional model Violin with bow for $4.00. Books on Chinese and Mongolian history sold for .50 cents.

The Chinese people had no idea of value and being a communist country they had no reason to.

Everything was different in those early days. In the summertime we would go to an outdoor food market, not to buy, but to observe. You could purchase apples for 2 Juan (about 1/3 of a penny or less) or a bloated dead rat (not gutted) for about the same price, for that nights dinner.

We were touring a city somewhere in the Chinese interior one day and since I had been to that particular city before I elected to stay near the air conditioned bus. I had just stepped out of the bus to have a cigarette (which I used to enjoy in those days) when I was approached by a dirty faced little boy of about 4 years of age. He was carrying his little sister who was even dirtier than he! It was a struggle for him to keep himself on his feet as he was not really strong enough to carry her. My driver was having a cigarette as well and he spoke broken English. The little boy staggered towards me and stopped looking up at me with his bright eyes and said something in Chinese that I did not understand. I looked at my driver and he said "the little boy would like to know if you would be interested in buying his little sister for 10 Juan". (about 2 1/2 cents American currency). I had to decline no matter how adorable the tiny dirty faced little girl was. It was not unusual to be taken to a place they called a hotel in those days that was nothing more than a co-educational bunk house. Being the tour director I was given the suite which consisted of three single wood frame beds with a wood mattress and a sheet. No pillow and no bathroom. Have you ever tried to sleep on a wood platform? Thank goodness it was summertime because I was trying to decide if I was to lay on the sheet or cover myself with it. I ended up using my rolled up slacks as a pillow and covered myself with the sheet. The bath room was primitive to say the least! It was a simple concrete ditch about 12 feet long, with a small trickle of water flowing towards the low end with not nearly enough force to wash any human waste away. The stench was terrible! There was no paper of any kind for wiping so you had to "make do" with your linen handkerchief or your socks. It was then you also discovered there was no water anywhere but that which was flowing in the concrete ditch so washing hands was out of the question. We stayed in that village for three days and it was not uncommon to enter the "bathroom" to find 5 or 6 Chinese men squatting like baseball catchers all in a row, "doing their business" and chatting up a storm. One could not help but laugh hysterically at a situation such as this but this was China in the late 70's.

There were very few automobiles in China in those days and the ones that were there were owned by the government. The operators of those automobiles were trained drivers that chauffeured government officials around. The main source of transportation for the Chinese people was the bicycle and there were millions upon millions of them. Heavy loads of freight were hauled in a two wheeled wooden wagon pulled by a donkey or a horse, and sometimes even by a woman. The more successful communes had big (what we call) 'garden tractors' and the driver of those two wheeled motor driven vehicles would sit on the trailer he was pulling and steer the garden tractor with the handle bars much like a bicycle.

The Japanese government was ahead of the American government because they began doing business with their once hated enemy long before President Nixon visited China in the mid 70's and opened the doors of China. Do you remember the term "the iron curtain"? Regardless of what you thought of President Nixon he had a wonderful talent in "breaking the ice" to our once sworn enemy, and he did.

Long before Americans ever visited China, Japan made peace with them and seeing that China was determined to become a powerful country the Japanese introduced them to the idea of tourism. They first acquired a contract to sell them modern and air conditioned tour buses. By doing so they also volunteered to provide driver training to selected Chinese garden tractor drivers. Before long the Japanese people were touring China and this occurred just before the Americans finally decided to bury the hatchet and become friendly.

The need for paved roadways became obvious to the Chinese government officials and to accomplish this endeavor they needed multitudes of manpower. We, (some of the first American visitors to China) got to see this road building process in action. You have never seen so many wheel barrows and shovels and tampers in your life. They had huge metal tanks and many Chinese workers mixing blacktop (hot tar and chipped stone). Other workers were shoveling the mixed blacktop into the wheel barrows and the driver of the wheel barrow would push his heavy load to where it needed to be dumped while more Chinese workers raked it out into a smooth layer of hot blacktop. Still more Chinese workers with flat metal tampers on the end of an iron pole were tamping the blacktop into a compacted mass of pavement. They could cover a four lane highway about a mile per day and they had thousands of miles to go! It one point I mentioned to my local Chinese interpreter that in America we had machines that could do all that work automatically. His response was, "maybe so but look how many people you would make unemployed if we did that". He had a good point!

On yet another occasion I watched as hundreds of strong Chinese men with little more clothing than a pair of pants and a pair of shoes carried on their backs (protected by a hemp mat) huge boulders that must have weighed 150 to 200 pounds each. They were tied up with a length of rope and carried from where the donkey drawn cart dropped them near the river as these men carried them one by one down the bank and loaded then on to a barge. The barge was then towed out to a designated spot on the river and one side of the barge was flooded causing it to roll on to its side dumping the load of boulders to the bottom. They were building a bridge to span the river and these huge boulders were for the pilings on which the bridge was to be built.

They have advanced their country from the primitive times in the 70's to what today is probably one of the most modern countries in the world. The have accomplished this in a matter of 30 years but I might mention they had the help and guidance of America and of course Japan.

Yes, they indeed were the good old days!

CHAPTER 29

Terrorism! A close call

The year was 1984 when I was contracted to lead a group of 32 people to tour three countries, the Philippines, Hong Kong and mainland China. It was springtime and a lovely time for traveling in the areas we were scheduled to visit. Our first stop for five days was Manila, the capital of the Philippines. The Filipino people are gracious and dearly love American's, especially the younger generation of Filipino's. It was not unusual for children the age of 6 to 12 to salute us as we walked by in a gesture taught to them by the generation of Filipinos that appreciated the efforts the American GI made to free their country from the Japanese occupation. They were of course way to young for memories of that time but it was obvious that schooling was teaching Philippine History. I for one am glad, the young generation of Filipino's will grow up loving Americans when the children of so many other countries will not.

It was a fine group I was leading, with many couples of middle age, as well as a few single women and a couple of single men. We visited the Rizal museum in Manila as well as the remains of the ocean side prison where so many of our brave American soldiers gave up their lives in world warII. We visited Pagsanjan Falls, a two hour drive north of Manila where we spend a delightful day being paddled up stream over rapids by a couple of strong Filipino boat men. When we arrived at the falls we were served a cold beverage and spent an hour or more there enjoying the awesome and mighty water falls. We watched as some local men enjoy a balute (which is a fully formed goose still inside the egg) that has been buried in limestone under the hot sun of the Philippines for 1000 days. It tastes just like deviled eggs we eat here in the states but you still have to deal with the tiny feathers that get caught between your teeth. (at least this is what I am told). I had a standing offer of $100.00 if I would eat one but I was never got that hungry nor did I need the hundred dollars that bad!

After a day of shopping and relaxation we were back on a smaller plane and heading for a city in the southern part of the Philippine islands called Zamboanga. Zamboanga is located in the province of Mindanao. Our hotel was the brand new Zamboanga Plaza Hotel which was built on a side hill of a rather large mountain overlooking the south pacific ocean. It was a spectacular location for a hotel with the most stunning view of an island that seemed to be afloat on the bright blue south pacific, a short distance off shore. The island is surrounded with pink sand beaches caused by the red coral and the water was as blue as could be and the island is dense with green palms and evergreens.

The air terminal in Zamboanga, was very primitive compared to the hotel and was built in the fashion of a tin Quonset hut, probably left over from world war II. After landing we were escorted to a waiting bus for our short ride to our hotel. The rest of the day was free but since we arrived there late in the afternoon we opted to enjoy happy hour before dinner at the hotel. We were all still suffering somewhat from the jet lag of the Trans pacific flight from Seattle to San Francisco to Honolulu to Manila. (an 18 hour flight time plus several hours of layover).

We all retired to our rooms early and were in for a good night's sleep. I am an early riser and as usual was awake and brewing my morning coffee in the coffee maker provided in each room for the guests. As is custom in most foreign countries a newspaper is shoved under you room door at about 5:30 AM and as I was sitting back to read the morning paper I thought I heard an occasional gunshot in the distance. Probably my imagine, I thought as I read on about local elections taking place and the weather was expected to be hot and dry. About 6:30 AM I made my way down to the lobby and noticed armed guards standing in the open entry of the lobby. That was not too unusual as the Philippine's were under martial law with president Marcos as president. What seemed unusual to me was the obvious young age of the guards standing around holding AK-47's. They appeared to be in their early teens!

Soon my group was gathering in the coffee shop for their morning breakfast and at 9 AM we boarded our bus for a city tour. There was no stops in the city but soon we were driving on a beach front road and we came to an area where there were houses built over the water on stilts. The bus parked and we disembarked and walked down the beach following our local guide as he made his way up a 2 inch by 12 inch plank to a walkway out to these houses on stilts. There were no guard rails and we were all a bit nervous as we walked between these flimsy houses built on stilts. Several mothers were sitting outside their doorways nursing new born infants in the morning sunlight and children of all ages came running up to us saluting us having learned how to do that from the American soldiers that occasionally visit the Mindanao area.

It was a delightful morning until the local guide began telling us the customs of the water people. The first thing a new born baby experiences after birth is a dunking in the South Pacific Ocean. He is thrown into the water from the walkway in front of his parent's house. If he comes to the surface and rolls on his back so he can breathe he is considered a strong baby and worthy to be rescued and live a normal life. If he is so unlucky as to rise to the surface and not roll on his back then he will drown and he does!!! No rescue for him or her because they believe he will be weak and susceptible to all decease's so they allow the infant to drown. How very sad we all felt having learned that tragic tradition. We paid special attention to the children of these water people and the infants being breast fed and admired the fight they have within themselves to stay alive. We all returned the salute we were given by these little ones as we left them for our next adventure.

Our bus proceeded along the beach road for several more miles when we came to a pier where several boats called Banca's were tied up. We came to a stop and off shore a mile or two we could see the island with the pink sand and green trees that we admired from our hotel on the hill. These banca's were made of hollowed out logs and had an outrigger on one side. It was big enough to accommodate all 32 of us with room left over for even more. It was powered by an old outboard engine that barked, sputtered and smoked and we joked about the possibility of having to swim all the way back to the mainland if this engine were to let us down. When we arrived safely on the island we were told there would be a lobster feast if they had caught one in their trap the night before and it would be a Filipino Bar-B-Q feast. A pit was dug in the beautiful pink sand and hot coals were dumped into it. The lobster trap yielded a huge lobster bigger than anything I had ever seen before! It was coal black and the tail alone was about 24 to 26 inches long and about 10 to12 inches in diameter at the widest. The boatman wrapped the entire lobster in many banana leaves and placed it on top of the hot coals and covered the pit with sand. He had bought buckets of lumpia and salads as well as cold drinks on ice. One of the girls asked if I would walk with her along the beach as she wanted to collect some sea shells so I agreed. We must have walked a half mile or more and we found a nautilus shell. They are spectacular and extremely fragile and how she was going to keep it in one piece for the balance of the trip was beyond my comprehension. About 10 feet past the area she found the nautilus I spied an oyster shell that seemed slightly open. I picked it up and reached for my pocket knife. The tide was going out and a fresh oyster or clam would taste good even without any sauce. It smelled fresh! With a few slices I was able to open it and to my amazement inside was a giant black pearl!!! I stuck it in my pocket and the young lady and I began the long walk back to our campsite and the Bar-B-Q. As we were walking I heard a familiar sound I had not heard since I was a child. It was the drone of a radial head airplane engine common on world war II fighter planes. Where I was born and spent my first 15 years of life was not real far from the Willow Grove Navel Air Base in Pennsylvania and our house was under the flight path of a lot of those fighter planes and other military aircraft. I looked to my left where the sound was coming from and could see our beautiful hotel in the distance across the blue water and partway up the side hill. Sure enough there was a P-51 fighter plane in a dive behind our hotel. The plane pulled up abruptly and I saw a tree rise from the ground with a lot of dust and dirt flying, followed by a tremendous "BOOM". My pace quickened as we hurried back to join up with the rest of my group. When we arrived back at camp I took the local guide aside and asked what was going on. He smiled and said "no problem, the army is practicing"! I said "WHAT", did you see how close that was to the hotel??? He replied that I should not worry the military were very good at aiming! Somehow that answer did not fit, but the rest of the group must have taken his answer earlier as the truth and they seemed at ease with what was going on. Not me! This was not normal. We continued to hear gun shots and cannon fire and the delicious lobster did not ease my angst as planes kept flying over as the distant sounds of war continued.

Sometime later, our stomachs full of lobster, lumpia, salad and San Migel beer we climbed back into the banca and made our way back to the bus with the old engine still barking, sputtering and spewing smoke. We boarded the bus and headed for our hotel. I asked the group to stay inside the hotel because there were many poisonous snakes in the surrounding area. I did not want to tell them of my real suspicions but what I said seemed to sink in and I knew I got their attention. I hung around the lobby looking like I was busy with paper work while making sure no one went outside. By 10 PM all were in their rooms and the gunfire was continuing. Again I went to the front desk and inquired about all the shooting and I got the same answer I had gotten from my local guide. Just military practice! Baloney!!! I spent a restless night with little sleep. We were to be two more days in Zamboanga but I sure did not look forward to that.

I was up at four AM and there was still an occasional gunshot heard in the distance. I made the coffee and picked up the morning paper from under my door. I sat down on the davenport and looked at the front page. I was still settling in when I suddenly was on my feet, my heart pounding and my knees turning weak! The headlines read "ZAMBOANGA CITY UNDER SIEGE". Without reading any further I ran out of my room and ran down the hallway grabbing the newspapers out from under the doorway of my group member's doors.

After retrieving all the papers I took them to my room and sat down to read the details of the article. Terrorists connected to the Al Quada organization are attempting to capture American tourists that are visiting Zamboanga. So far the Philippine Air Force and ground forces are able to deflect the attacks and there are many casualties, both in the military as well as the insurgents.

I raced to the front desk and demanded to know the facts. There were about 15 armed military men standing by the open entrance of the hotel and military vehicles outside the door. I was furious! I demanded that we leave the hotel as soon as the group awakened. To my surprise they said that arrangements for our departure back to Manila were already made. I was filled with anger! For years it had been a known fact that terrorists were common in Mindanao but for the past several years the Philippine government insisted that the terrorists had been defeated and travel to that area was again safe! NOT! Anyway we finished breakfast and boarded our bus and with a military escort we made our way to the airport and a waiting airplane for our ride to Manila. The group was given a free day of shopping for sarongs and souvenirs and I went directly to Philippine Airlines and demanded to know why a group was allowed to go to Mindanao in the first place. I was surprised at their answer! It was 'Mr Rosenberger, we take care of our guests and no one was hurt were they'? I just shock my head and walked out. The following day we boarded a plane and flew to the safe harbor of Hong Kong.

Tourism has been closed in Mindanao ever since and even today it is considered unsafe travel for any foreigners. The beautiful brand new Zamboanga Plaza Hotel is no longer in business and is wasting away to ruins.

CHAPTER 30

Night Life in Tokyo

There were times when tourism was extremely busy. On such occasions when my previous group would end its trip in Hong Kong, I would say goodbye to the group there at Kai Tak Airport as they were heading back to the states. I would then catch a flight to Tokyo to meet a new group that would be arriving in a couple days. On one such occasion instead of heading for the nearest bar in Tokyo to pass the time I decided to visit a Tokyo Casino.

I must first tell you a little bit about Japanese bars. They serve Saki and they serve Sapporo Whiskey and they serve Sapporo Beer. They also sell American booze but at a very premium price. With a lot of free time in Tokyo I decided to save money and purchase the whole bottle of Glenlevit Scotch from the bar. They make a brass name plate with a small brass bracelet that hangs on the neck of the bottle with the owners name on it. When I return on any consequent visits to Tokyo I simply ask for my bottle and a sweet little Japanese girl brings your bottle to your table, falls to her knees at your feet and pours your drink the way you like it. In my case it was on the rocks with water as chaser. This service was by tip only since I have already paid dearly for the scotch. I liked this arrangement!

Anyway, back to the casino experience. I am normally not a gambling man but since I had a very financially successful previous trip the extra money was burning a hole in my pocket. I grabbed a cab at the Akasaka Prince Hotel where I was staying and off to the casino I went. Gambling was not legal in Japan but they did have pin ball machines. Unlike our American pin ball machines which are more or less horizontal with a slight angle to allow the stainless steel ball to gravitate towards the bottom end, Japanese pin ball machines are vertical. Also instead of pulling a plunger back and letting it 'fly' to send the ball on its way in Japan the machines had a dial that increased or decreased the speed of the ball when the button was pressed to send it on its way. I was not having very good luck with this method of playing and the fellow playing next to me noticed my failed efforts. He took a 50 yen coin and asked me if he could help me. I said of course and he proceeded to slide the coin under the dial that regulated the speed of the ball. Now this Casino was a noisy place with bells ringing all the time from the various and many machines. My Japanese helper was adjusting the speed of the ball on my machine and he must have hit the correct speed as all of a sudden bells and whistles started ringing in my machine and stainless steel balls were falling out of the machine into a plastic bucket on the floor. The bells kept ringing and the balls kept falling and suddenly another Japanese guy came running with more buckets!!! Before long I had 5 buckets of stainless steel balls about the size of marbles! By now I was collecting an audience and all the Japanese men were standing there and patting me on the back and laughing and clapping. I ended up with 7 buckets of stainless steel marbles of which I had no idea what I was going to do with. The manager of the Casino came by and took me by the arm and led me to an area away from the machines while several helpers brought my 7 buckets of stainless steel marbles. The manager began dumping my balls into what must have been a counting machine and when the last ball fell through the grate, the machine printed out something in Japanese that must have said '7 buckets of stainless steel balls'. As he was escorting me to the exit I asked him what I was supposed to do with the piece of paper he gave me? He motioned to one of his helpers and he said follow me in broken English. It was after midnight and we were walking down a very dark ally and I was thankful I was in Japan and not Elizabeth, New Jersey! Finally we came to a stairs on the sidewalk leading to the second floor. We climbed to the top and knocked on the door. Instead of the door opening a tiny little door opened up in the door and my helper asked for the piece of paper I had gotten from the Casino manager. He passed it through the tiny little window and the window closed. We stood there in silence and I finally said 'now what'? He responded 'one moment please'. Soon we heard shuffling behind the big door and sure enough it opened allowing light from inside to pour out on to the deck we were standing on. He was carrying a huge cardboard box and he handed it to me and went back inside and closed the door. In darkness we made our way down the stairs and onto the street below. The box was heavy and awkward but I was glad to be back on the street and I headed for the nearest street light. My helper had long since disappeared and I was alone with the huge box. Finally I spied a cab coming my way and I flagged him down.

We arrived back at the Akasaka Prince Hotel and when the cabbie opened the trunk a bellhop came running to help me with the huge box. He placed it on a dolly and followed me into the elevator and back to my room. I was dying to know what was in the box. When I finally reached my room I was able to open my huge prize! What a surprise it was too. The huge cardboard box was filled with 144 individual smaller boxes of Sunny Maid Raisins! If I wouldn't have been so confused and concerned about what to do with all the raisins I might have found some humor in it but humor was not in my mind. I hauled the carton of raisins back down to the lobby and found my cabbie asleep in his cab outside the main entrance of the hotel. After waking him I asked him to take me back to the same place he had picked me up and back in the trunk went the huge box. I found my way back to the stairs on the side walk and up to the deck where I once again knocked on the door. I told the guy through the tiny window I did not want the raisins and he opened the big door and took the raisins inside and closed the door. I started down the stairs and was just at the bottom when he called after me. He was holding something. I went back up the stairs and he handed me a hand full of Japanese yen.

When I got back to the Akasaka Prince and counted the yen it was the equivalent of $46.00 US dollars.

That was my very first and also my very last experience with gambling anywhere not just in Japan. I never did like raisins anyway!

CHAPTER 31

The Horse Dance

It was the mid 80's when I took advantage of an opportunity to go on a cruise. Instead of going back to the states for R&R I chose to instead take a cruise sailing out of Singapore with ports of call in both Indonesia but also Penang and Kuala Lumpur in Malaysia. The ship was named the Rasa Sayang and it was owned by a Norwegian company called American Norwegian lines. It was a beautiful old cruise ship, originally christened the "Bergensfjord" when it cruised under the German flag.

Now, under the name of Rasa Sayang, it sailed out of Singapore to destinations in Indonesia and Malaysia. Her officers were all Norwegian which of course included Captain Oley Christian Bjornstad. He was a strikingly good looking man, very dignified, and he and I became very good friends. The deck crew, were all Singaporean, known for their hard working ethics. The cabin crew, were all Malaysian which have some of the most beautiful women in the world.

I had purposely arrived 2 days early in Singapore (before the scheduled sailing of the Rasa Sayang) so I could have a couple days to relax, shop and visit friends. I checked into the gorgeous, world famous, Raffles Hotel, the home of many American movie legends, such as Humphrey Bogart, Audrey Hepburn, Julie Andrews, Clark Gable, the entire cast of the "Sound Of Music" and names I have long since forgotten. There is nothing in this world more romantic than sitting in the courtyard of the Raffles Hotel on a moonlit night, sipping on a Singapore Sling with a gorgeous Singaporean girl.

The day of the sailing finally came and I was besides myself with excitement. I grabbed a taxi and must have been the first passenger to come aboard. I was met at the gangway by June (a beautiful Singaporean girl who happened to be the cruise director). She asked my name and when I told her she went to the manifest and suddenly she acted as though I was her very best friend. She told me the captain had wished that I should occupy one of the two suite's on the ship! WOW!!! What a surprise! She had porters take my baggage to my suite while she took me on a tour of the ship. We saw the entire ship including the four bars, three dining rooms the workout room the casino the swimming pool, the library and sitting room and finally she took me on my private elevator to my suite. It was unbelievable! The room was huge compared to the single and double rooms she had shown me during my tour. I had a huge king size bed, my own wet bar completely stocked with every kind of booze that money could buy. I had my own living room with TV a desk for writing letters and eating cabin service meals. There was a full bath room with tub and shower. As an added feature when I opened my cabin door and looked out I was a floor above the grand ball room and there was a spiral staircase that arc'd its way right up to my Cabin door. By simply walking out my penthouse door I could walk to the railing and look down on the dance floor. Or from inside my penthouse I could enter my private elevator and choose which floor I wished to exit. I had a private balcony accessed from the reading room of my suite. My elevator was only accessible by me though a programed card that I inserted into a card slot to open the doors. I was treated like a king!

We were still at the dock and people were still loading so I took a shower and got into my bathing suit and went for a swim. It was hot outside. At about 4 PM I heard the announcement over the loud speaker that we would be sailing in 30 minutes. I went back to my room and dressed in a shirt and slacks. From there I made my way to the promenade deck to watch the departure. The whistle was blowing and the con fete was flowing as we slipped silently with the help of a few tug boats into the South Indian Ocean. Soon we were free from the tugs and on our way. I stood by the railing for what must have been hours watching flying fish which I had never seen before. Slowly Singapore disappeared from view and I returned to my room. To my surprise there was a fruit basket full of every kind of exotic fruit plus a bottle of champagne nestled in a bucket of ice on my coffee table. There was a note from Captain Oley Christian Bjornstadt welcoming me aboard and inviting me to join him at the captain's table for dinner that night. What an honor! Very few people ever get an invitation to join the captain for dinner at HIS table!!! Thank goodness I owned a tuxedo which I had made for me on one of my trips to Hong Kong in previous years.

Captain Bjornstadt and I got along famously and he enjoyed my sense of humor, especially when I suggested the matre'd would make a better undertaker then a dinner host. Captain Bjornstadt roared in laughter and whispered that he agreed with me.

After dinner I returned to my room to watch TV. There was a note on my coffee table that a singles mingle party would be taking place at 9 PM in the Grand Ball Room. I had no intention of going to a singles mingle party but I must admit I was curious as to how many single people were on the cruise. About 10:30 my curiosity got the best of me and I opened the cabin door and peeked over the railing. There was a man of at least 80 years of age and a young man of possibly 16 years of age. All the rest were women that ranged from early 20's to their 40's, and there had to be 50 of them. They all were drinking heavily and I could tell from their accents they were all from Australia. (Australia is just 800 miles from Singapore.) Australian women vacation by themselves and so do their husbands I learned later.

Two days of sailing and we were approaching Jakarta, Indonesia for a one day stop. I had been to Jakarta many times before so I did not go ashore but stayed aboard and kept the bar tender busy. When that got to boring I went for a swim and by then it was dinner time and back in my tux with a different colored cummerbund and bow tie for dinner with Captain Bjornstadt again. (of the 14 day cruise I had dinner at the captain's table 10 times.)

Our second port of call was Bali, Indonesia, one of my most favorite places in the world. Since there is no port in Bali we anchored off shore and went ashore on a tender boat. I had to go ashore just to have my grilled lobster for dinner that night.

Whenever I went to Bali I always saved one night's dinner for grilled lobster. For $3.50 how can you not enjoy a giant lobster tail with a baked potato and green salad? After dinner I made my way back to the ship and took a swim before bedtime.

When I awoke next morning we were again underway and our destination was Surabaya, Indonesia. A word of advice here. If you ever get the opportunity to visit Surabaya, DON'T GO!!! There is absolutely nothing at all to do there. There is no beach. The food is terrible. There is nothing to see of any interest, but they do have a horse dance. Having been a fan of horses all my life I wanted to see the horse dance and since I had never been to Surabaya before I decided to go ashore and see it. OMG! About 30 of us went in a bus to see this horse dance and we arrived at a pavilion type bldg. We went inside and I thought they had to have very small horses because the ceiling was so low. Soon a man walked in leading a young man on a leash or lead strap as it were. They did not speak English. The older man took a feather from one of his pockets and started rubbing the nose of the young man with this feather. He was talking the entire time but we had no idea what he was saying. Soon the eyes of the young man began to roll back in his head and he started drooling at the corner of his mouth. About the same time he started pawing at the ground with his foot and he whinnied just exactly like a horse. The older man reached into a cardboard box and pulled out a hand full of green grass that was at least 15 to 18 inches long. The young man started eating it like a horse and he continued to paw the ground and whinnie like a horse. I could not believe my eyes as he ate the entire bunch of grass and he was obviously in a very deep trance. He was now jumping around like a wild horse and pawing the ground like crazy. This had been going on for about 30 minutes when the older man said something to the young man and the young man sat down on a chair as the old man brought another cardboard box and this one was half full of light bulbs. There was a vacant look in the young man's eyes as the older man handed him the first light bulb. I did not know a human being could open their mouth that wide but he took that light bulb into his mouth and you could see him putting pressure on it until finally it popped and he began chewing the glass. He chewed it up and swallowed it and then took another bulb and repeated the process. After about 4 light bulbs were completely consumed the older man took the same feather he had earlier and began rubbing the nose of the young man. This time he was talking in a milder manner and a softer voice and soon the young man began coming out of the deep trance he had been in. I was touched when I saw him begin to cry as he was coming to as if he had not wanted to do that but woke up realizing he had done it again. When he realized there were all these people watching him he stopped crying and began picking small pieces of broken glass from his tongue. I sat there in shock for quite a long time not believing I had just seen what I saw. Then it was back to the bus and the ride back to the dock and the Rasa Sayang. I was never so glad to be back in civilization as I was that moment.

I went to the bar and had a couple drinks and skipped dinner completely.

The following morning when I awoke and stepped out onto my balcony I discovered we were again underway and had left Surabaya behind us. It was a three day cruise back to Singapore where we docked for less than 2 hours and were off again cruising now towards Kuala Lumpur, Malaysia. The next morning we were approaching the port of Kuala Lumpur when there was a knock on my penthouse door. I opened the door to find a stewardess there and she handed me an envelope that was marked "from Captain Bjornstadt". I thanked her with a small tip and opened the envelope. Inside was a hand written note from Captain Bjornstadt. I learned that while we had disembarked some passengers in Singapore the day before we had also taken on board the owners of the Rasa Sayang. Eric Svenson was the primary owner of American Norwegian Lines. I was invited to join the Captain, the first officer, the owner, Mr. Svenson and several male friends of Mr. Svenson for lunch when we docked in Kuala Lumpur. We were all to meet in "the Ships Wheel" bar after the docking.

I wasted no time as we were docking and arrived first at the "Ships Wheel" bar.

Thirty minutes later I was joined by Captain Bjormstadt and his accompanying owner and friends. After introductions all around we disembarked the ship and with two taxi's we went on a wild ride through the streets of Kuala Lumpur. About 20 minutes later we arrived at a deserted beach of white sand, blue water and green palm trees. On the beach there was a covered pavilion with about 8 beautiful Malaysian girls in their sarongs waiting for us. Behind the girls stood several Malaysian young men and they were holding wicker baskets of some kind. We were welcomed with refreshing cold drinks by the eight girls. We sat under the pavilion, out of the heat from the hot tropical sun. The table was set for lunch but there was no food in sight. Just dishes silverware napkins etc. The three young Malaysian men took their baskets and disappeared into the South China Sea wearing their snorkel tubes. There was a small bonfire burning some distance away from the pavilion and we sat around being lavished with affection and service from the girls.

Soon the three men returned from the ocean with their baskets over flowing with shrimp and lobster. They walked to us to show us their catch that was still flapping their tails and then went to the fire and began cooking our dinner.

It was not long afterwards that lunch was served with baked potato's, salad and the freshest and most delicious lobster and shrimp that I can remember. We devoured our lunch and the three men were back in the water catching more seafood. It was probably three or four hours later that we finally bid our beautiful hostesses goodbye and after hugs and kisses for each of us we were off to the Rasa Sayang once again.

The following day we were once again underway and this time our destination was Penang, Malaysia. I declined the opportunity to go ashore as I had been to Penang many times and had no reason to visit it yet another time. Instead I spent the time swimming in the ships pool and enjoying a couple of exotic drinks. The following day we were off once again into the South China Sea and homeward bound back to Singapore.

I must say it was a bit sad to say goodbye to my new friends and the Rasa Sayang when we docked back in Singapore. This time I checked into the brand new Pacifica Hotel with all the bathrooms decorated with imported pink marble from Italy on each and every one of its 102 floors. At the time it was the highest hotel in the world and it may still be I don't know.

Then it was back to the airport for the multi-leg flights back to the good old USA. What an adventure!!!

CHAPTER 32

Indonesian zoo

During one of my trips into Indonesia my group was taken to a zoo at dusk. They had infra red lights that glowed enough for us to see about 8 or 10 Komoto Dragons feeding on a deer carcass the zoo keepers fed them. I had seen this spectacle before so I wondered away from the group and was investigating other parts of the zoo grounds alone. I came across a lone elephant that was tied to a tree by his hind leg. He was enormous! I have seen many elephants in real life in Thailand, Malaysia and even in the Philippines but I had never seen one quite as large as this one. I wondered how close I dared come to him because he was not inside an enclosure but just tied to a tree by his hind leg. The elephant seemed friendly enough but yet I remained a bit skeptical, because of the enormous power a beast of this size must have. I closed the distance between us to about 12 feet standing approximately by his mid section. Not wanting to be kicked by a hind foot or grabbed by his powerful trunk I felt I was at the safest place I could be. I was dressed for dinner as that was our next stop after leaving the zoo. In the darkness I saw the elephant lower his trunk into a puddle of muddy water and with a subtle flick of his trunk he showered me with about a cup full of liquid mud. I did not expect that and I did not see it coming and it happened very fast. I could never have gotten away quick enough to avoid the muddy baptism. I took a step backwards and I swear the elephant was laughing at me as his head was bobbing up and down. I laughed too as suddenly it was funny! If I had not had that instinctive fear of such a large animal I would have gone to the mud puddle and threw some at him as payback but my better judgment led me back to my group instead. Just another experience of some pleasant memories from the past.

CHAPTER 33

Sir Walter Bernard

I t was in 1988 I believe when I received a phone call from Tyler Tanaka in Los Angeles, California. Seldom, if ever do I get a phone call from him and he is the owner of Japan and Orient Tours, one of the land operator companies which I was contracted with. The purpose of his personal call was of great importance he claimed and it was a request that I agree to accept a group of very senior citizens from the east coast for a 19 day tour of three countries. He claimed he had a reason for requesting that I alone should be responsible for this trip. Not knowing or completely understanding the urgency in his voice I reluctantly agreed to accept the group. He thanked me gratefully and told me the profiles would be mailed to me that same day. The profiles were photos of each and every passenger complete with information on their age, birthday, health problems and addresses.

Two days later I received the express envelope containing the profiles. The group consisted of 21 people, which included a married couple, a single man and 18 women. The age range was from 72 to 98 years of age. I nearly fainted! This group was going to be a big problem! To be honest it was like taking a group of people, each of whom had one foot already in the grave and the other on a slick banana peel. Our first destination was Japan and that country did not worry me. It was the following two countries that had me worried sick. (mainland China and Hong Kong). These two countries (unlike Japan) want you to see as much as they can possibly show you in the shortest time possible. People of such vintage cannot be expected to keep up with the pace they set.

It was already too late to decline the group so I proceeded to memorize the photos with the names so that I could recognize them at the airport where I was to meet them in Seattle the day of our journey. I was practiced at this procedure as I did this for every group I ever escorted. The only problem I ever had was when a woman of her 50's would send a photo of herself on graduation day from high school. Sometime they were hard to identify!

The day of departure arrived and I was at SeaTac Airport early to meet all the incoming flights carrying my group members. Most of the ladies were from New York and they all came on the same flight. They seemed shocked and confused when I greeted them all by their first names. Walter Bernard, the youngest of the entire group, at 72 years of age, was the last to arrive and he was coming from Atlanta Georgia. We had an hour and 45 minutes before our flight to Japan was to leave so I took the group to the nearest bar (inside the terminal) and hosted a short cocktail party. They all had a multitude of questions and I knew this was going to be an unusually hard trip for me. The flight from Seattle to Tokyo is a relatively short flight as international flights go and it is just 9 hours long. The confusion is that although it is just a nine hour flight we do cross the International Date Line on our flight there. Our flight leaves Seattle at 11:15 AM on a Monday morning and we fly in daylight all the way to Japan, arriving there at 4:00 PM on Tuesday. Younger people can more easily accept the explanation of crossing the international dateline but for people of this advanced age it requires additional time consuming verbal comforting until they finally accept my word that we have gained a day. I also begin to inform them as to what to expect when they arrive in Japan. On this particular trip we stayed at the Palace Hotel in the Maranuchi district of Tokyo. This hotel is very close to the Imperial Palace of Japan (their White House).

Upon arrival at the Hotel I lead the group to the front desk and I check each and every one in to their pre assigned rooms. I distribute their room keys and their meal coupons and advise them to try to stay awake until at least 9 or 10 O'clock PM. I know they are exhausted from the long flight and the one and a half hour bus ride from Narita Airport to downtown Tokyo. I also inform them the bus for our city tour tomorrow will be at the main entrance at precisely 9:00 AM the following morning. Inevitably one or more of the more senior ladies will come to me in the bar later and ask me what time the 9 O'clock bus leaves. Single ladies no matter what age, for some reason always have silly questions like that. They are lonely and want companionship with someone, anyone!

Well, the following morning my deepest fears became reality! I am an early riser and became that way from escorting groups through foreign countries. Japanese people are very polite when they are in their own country and they are precisely on time! The Hotel cafe' opened at 7 AM every morning. I usually have my morning coffee in my room before I go to breakfast at 7 AM. When I approached the cafe' I could see that Mr. Bernard was already inside the cafe' but the glass doors were still locked. It was obvious that he was having a heated argument with the waiter. I knocked on the glass door and the waiter, looking quite relieved ran to the door and unlocked it for me and allowed me to come in locking the door behind me as it was not yet 7 AM. I asked Walter what was going on and he said where the hell are we Merrill, these people are speaking a funny language! I explained that we were in Japan and I asked how he got into the cafe before 7 AM. He responded that if he was not allowed to come in he was going to the hotel manager. I can assure you that in Japan if they say the restaurant opens at 7 AM that is precisely what they mean. All personnel inside the cafe' could be ready for business and standing by the door but the door will not be unlocked until the second hand reaches 12 at precisely 7 AM.

I talked the waiter into allowing us to stay in the cafe for the 4 minutes remaining until the second hand reached 12 at 7 AM. I then left Walter and greeted the remaining group members as they slowly trickled into the cafe.

When I returned to the area where I had left Walter he was again in a heated argument with a waiter. I interrupted and inquired what was going on. He said 'they want some kind of coupon from me'. I told him that I gave him an envelope the night before with the coupons and his room key. He said he did receive the envelope but there was only a room key inside. I found that very hard to believe so I asked him where the envelope was and he said it is probably in my waste basket. I then told the waiter to give him whatever he wanted for breakfast and I would take care of it. Well, that settled the breakfast problem but he also has lunch and dinner coupons in that envelope and I was not about to fight this situation every meal for the next five days in Japan. I sat down across the table from Walter and looked him in the eyes. I said Walter do you trust me. He said of course I do Merrill, you are the only friend I have. I said if you will give me your room key I will go there and try to locate the envelope and save you the trip. He graciously agreed and I ran to his room! He had made his bed not realizing that room service would come later and change sheets etc. I first went to his waste baskets but nothing was there. I was beginning to worry about Walter. He had no clothes in any of the drawers or the hanging closet so the only place left was his suit case. I hated to invade his privacy by opening his suit case but I felt I had no choice. Was I surprised when I opened it! His suit case was very heavy! When I opened the lid what I found was one pair of pants, one pair of socks, one shirt and one pair of under shorts. The rest of the case was filled to the top with all kinds of photographic equipment. No coupons! Now I was beginning to really worry about him. After one final search of the room I was satisfied that the coupons were not there so I made my way back to the cafe. Walter was busy eating his breakfast and I said Walter have you checked your pockets? He replied that he had and for some reason I reached across the table and inside his jacket to his inside chest pocket. I almost leaped for joy when I pulled out the envelope with his breakfast coupons still inside. But now I had a more serious problem. It was obvious to me that Walter was having a hard time remembering things so I asked him if I could keep his passport for him. He seemed very grateful and kept repeating how thankful he was to have me looking out for him. He gave me his passport and I decided to join him for the remainder of breakfast. My mind was churning with nightmares of Walter and his dilemma. I feared that Walter was senile. I finally got enough nerve to ask him if he was carrying any money. Without hesitation he replied that he had $400.00 in cash and $400.00 in traveler's checks. I told him I really cared about him and I wanted to protect him the best that I could. He kept thanking me for my kindness and then I asked him if he really trusted me. He said 'absolutely Merrill'. I explained to him that if he were to give me all his money I would give him a receipt witnessed by another member of the group and whenever he wanted some money I would give it to him and keep accounting of all the transactions. He seemed thrilled that I would do this for him and he handed the entire $800.00 in cash and checks over to me. I had Mr and Mrs. Belthaven witness the transaction and I sighed in relief!!!

This was the beginning of a trip I will never forget. Walter would forget from time to time where he was and would ask me why everyone was speaking a funny language. When I would remind him we were in Japan he would always strike his forehead with the ball of his hand and say 'oh dummy me'!

The Palace Hotel is directly across the street from the Imperial Palace, the home of the Emperor of Japan. The next exciting thing that occurred, that also included Walter was our last full day in Japan. That day was a free day for the group to do whatever they wanted to do. Not thinking about Walter (since his room key would tell anyone where he was staying) I had no fear since I still had his passport and his money. On days off like this I was free to visit some of my Japanese friends which I usually did and this day was no different. I always made it back to the hotel by 6 PM because dinner was served my group at 7 PM.

At 7 PM we all gathered at our table in the banquet room and all were there but Walter. I asked the mater'd to wait for 20 minutes before taking our order because one of my group members had not yet arrived. Twenty minutes came and went and still no Walter. I was beginning to worry but told the mater'd to go ahead and take our orders. I saved a seat next to myself for Walter should he show up. About 8 PM here came Walter with three of his camera's hanging from his neck. (As usual). He had to be a professional photographer at one time in his life. He had all kinds of cameras and every type of lens attachments you could possibly think of.

He pulled out his chair and settled down beside me and said boy Merrill, these police in this country are really strict! I nearly fainted, wondering and fearful of what he was about to tell me. What he said next nearly put me on the floor! He had gone across the street, with his photo equipment and walked right through the gate (forbidden) into the palace grounds. I guess the guards were so struck by his brazen approach and entrance they stood there none believing their eyes. In Walter's own words he said he saw a high point that would give him an advantage photographically so he walked to the top of that high point. He said the next thing he knew he was surrounded by policemen and they were mad! He said they all were talking a funny language but once they realized he was not going to hurt anybody they helped him set up his tripod and camera's. He said they even posed for a photo of themselves and then helped him repack all his gear. When he was all packed up they walked him right back to the hotel entrance.

I was beginning to find humor in all that Walter was doing and that made the trip a bit more interesting.

The following day it was back to the airport for our flight to Beijing, China. Some of the women in the group started feeling sorry for Walter and I noticed they were flanking him with one on each of his arms. On arrival in China I went immediately to the local guide and explained (to no avail) that this group must not be rushed as they were all very old people. We arrived in the afternoon so the rest of that day was free. The following morning it was off to the Ming tombs. By 1988 there were lots of brand new hotels (some were constructed by American contractors). All were very nice by this time. I think we were staying at the Beijing Hilton. As the day wore on I noticed that Walter with two ladies, one under each arm was moving slower and slower. I decided to walk behind him for a while and observe. It wasn't long before I got the distinct impression that Walter was enjoying the help of the two well-meaning ladies. After some time I got the two ladies alone without Walter and suggested they not help so much that I felt that Walter was taking advantage of their kindness. I asked for them to just try it for a while to see what happened. They agreed and sure enough it worked and the group began to pick up a little speed again. Still a lot slower than most groups but faster than a dead stop!

Every day I worried that someone in the group was going to get sick or have a heart attack. I had been guiding for many years by this time and had yet to lose one of my group members. From the time I met the group in Seattle I had been telling them to not eat a lot of fruit in the countries we were visiting. All through Japan I would remind them of that and in China it was even more important. The reason for this is because they pick their fruit fresh from the tree after it has ripened. In America for example we pick it all green and it ripens in the store or in your kitchen. In the orient and Southeast Asia it is always picked ripe and is far richer than our bodies are used to. It can and does cause diarrhea, BIG TIME!!! So far so good! No one has come down with the "trots". We still had Hong Kong to deal with and I was not going to stop my daily warnings about eating too much fruit. We finally said good bye to China after seeing the Great Wall, the Ming Tombs, the summer Palace and the Forbidden City. No China visit is complete without the mandatory stop at the "Friendship Store". The friendship stores are in most cities of China but Beijing has one of the biggest of its kind. It has items from furniture to kites and jewelry, not to mention musical instruments. Then it was off to the airport for our flight to Hong Kong.

After a spectacular landing in Hong Kong's famous kaitak airport we were bussed to the beautiful Meridian Hotel overlooking Hong Kong Harbor. For those of you that have never been to Hong Kong the now obsolete kaitak airport. What makes that airport so spectacular is the final approach. The runway extends out into the South China Sea and just before touchdown you are flying between two high rise apartment complexes. I have more than once landed there at night time to see women washing their dishes through the kitchen window as our plane passed them! Once you touch down it feels more like you have just landed on an aircraft carrier than an airport. The engines are reversed and full thrust is demanded as well as full braking as the runway is just too short for these modern new wide bodied aircraft. Over the years I have gotten to know a lot of airline pilots that fly into Hong Kong regularly. When asked why there are not more accidents at that airport they answer 'that is because every pilot that lands there knows that one small mistake and it's over'. Pilots take very special care when landing there.

Anyway here we were in one of my favorite places called Hong Kong. We were met by our local guides and bussed to our Hotel. Just 4 more days to go and we all fly back to the USA. I was really feeling pretty good about the group because no one died, no one got sick and no one even got diarrhea. I took my group to my favorite restaurant in the whole world, 'The Belvedere', also overlooking Hong Kong Harbor. I was greeted as usual by Peter the mater'd with Herro Misal Losenbelgel. (the Chinese have a difficult time pronouncing their "R"s and "L"s).

I had my favorite Chinese meal of King Prawns which are the size of lobster tail and just as good. They are served with the head still attached but I just eat the tail. The cooks love to have me visit because I never eat the heads, which they devour after I leave. When I am alone or with a lady friend I was always given my special window table where I could watch the Chinese sunset as the San Pans sail by with their colorful sails.

After an island tour and a little shopping it was our last day before heading home. I was so proud of myself that no one had gotten sick and I was sitting in the beautiful lobby bar enjoying a cocktail when here came Walter and he was walking funny! He was a bit pale and he said 'Merrill, I hate to tell you but I have the trots'. My heart sank! Why now Lord? I asked Walter if he could sit down and wait for me to return in 5 minutes and he said he could. I ran across the street and bought him a bottle of Kaopectate. When I returned he was still sitting there and I told him to go to his room and fill a glass to one inch and drink it down. Then I told him to take a nap and maybe he would feel better. So I saw him get in the elevator and I sat there in disappointment that my group had not been completely successful. I ordered another drink and was beginning to feel sorry for myself that I was unable to keep everyone healthy. When I looked up Walter was again walking towards me. He was still walking funny but this time he had a whitish ring around his mouth and he said 'Merrill, what did you tell me to do after I drank that stuff'? It was all I could do to keep from bursting into laughter. 'I said to take a short nap before dinner' and he again struck his forehead with the palm of his hand and said oh silly me as he headed for the elevator.

That evening we had our farewell to the Orient dinner. I toasted the group and thanked them for being such a wonderful group. Walter was there and he looked a lot better. He ate his meal and apparently he no longer had diarrhea. Then to my surprise he stood up and toasted me! It nearly brought tears to my eyes. When he finished his toast he ended it by saying that he heard there was a castle somewhere in England called Bernard Castle. He said next year I am going there and Merrill I want you by my side. "Will you be my guide"? I said "absolutely Sir Walter Bernard, absolutely!!!

The group was in for yet another surprise on the trip home. It is a 10 and one half hour flight, nonstop from Hong Kong to Seattle. Even though we left Hong Kong at 1:30 in the afternoon, on Monday, we will have seen two sunrises and one sunset and arrive in Seattle at 10:30 AM, Monday morning, before the time we left Hong Kong!

I will let you figure that one out.

P.S. I no sooner got home and in my house when my phone rang. It was Tyler Tanaka! He sounded very happy! He asked me how the group was and I told him it was great! He asked about Walter Bernard and I told him he made it all the way to Hong Kong but got diarrhea the second last day. He went on to tell me that Mr. Bernard was diagnosed with cancer but was never told about it. He was given 60 days to live and since he always wanted to go to the orient his family got together and financed his trip. Tyler said I knew if I gave this trip to you, that you would be the one that would bring him back alive and well. It was a tremendous compliment to me but I did ask Tyler not to give any more groups like that.

CHAPTER 34

China, The Early Days

C hina was a wonderful place to visit back in the late 70's. Not, that it is not a great place today, but it was so wild and totally innocent in those days. You could not purchase American products then and if you ran out of your American cigarettes you had two surprises! One was a nice surprise but the other was terrible. In those days a pack of American cigarettes cost around a dollar. On the other hand a pack of 20 cigarettes in China (Chinese tobacco) cost about .12 cents a pack, US equivalent! The taste, however of those cigarettes from China left a lot to be desired. Possibly if you rolled up the dirtiest pair of socks you ever saw, rolled it in paper and lit the end it just might give you the idea of what I am talking about. A half-gallon of Chivas Regal whiskey in the USA cost around $30.00 but a half gallon of Chinese Mao Tai was about $3.50 US equivalent. When you first open the bottle of Mao Tai, anyone within talking distance would immediately inquire as to what smells of dirty socks! Ah, the good old days! You could buy a professional model Violin with bow for $4.00. Books on Chinese and Mongolian history sold for .50 cents.

The Chinese people had no idea of value and being a communist country they had no reason to.

Everything was different in those early days. In the summertime we would go to an outdoor food market, not to buy, but to observe. You could purchase apples for 2 Juan (about 1/3 of a penny or less) or a bloated dead rat (not gutted) for about the same price, for that nights dinner.

We were touring a city somewhere in the Chinese interior one day and since I had been to that particular city before, I elected to stay near the air conditioned bus. I had just stepped out of the bus to have a cigarette (which I used to enjoy in those days) when I was approached by a dirty faced little boy of about 4 years of age. He was carrying his little sister who was even dirtier than he! It was a struggle for him to keep himself on his feet as he was not really strong enough to carry her. My driver was having a cigarette as well and he spoke broken English. The little boy staggered towards me and stopped looking up at me with his bright eyes and said something in Chinese that I did not understand. I looked at my driver and he said 'the little boy would like to know if you would be interested in buying his little sister for 10 Juan'. I had to decline no matter how adorable the tiny dirty faced little girl was. It was not unusual to be taken to a place they called a hotel in those days that was nothing more than a co-educational bunk house. Being the tour director I was given the suite which consisted of three single wood frame beds with a wood mattress and a sheet. No pillow and no bathroom. Have you ever tried to sleep on a wood platform? Thank goodness it was summertime because I was trying to decide if I was to lie on the sheet or cover myself with it. I ended up using my rolled up slacks as a pillow and covered myself with the sheet. The bath room was primitive to say the least! It was a simple concrete trench about 12 feet long, with a small trickle of water flowing towards the low end with not nearly enough force to wash any human waste away. The stench was terrible! There was no paper of any kind for wiping so you had to "make do" with whatever you had. It was then you also discovered there was no water anywhere but that which was flowing in the concrete trench so washing hands was out of the question. We stayed in that village for three days and it was not uncommon to enter the bathroom to find 5 or 6 Chinese men squatting like baseball catchers all in a row, "doing their business" and chatting up a storm or reading the newspaper. One could not help but laugh hysterically at a situation such as this but this was China in the late 70's.

There were very few automobiles in China in those days and the ones that were there were owned by the government. The operators of those automobiles were trained drivers that chauffeured government officials around. The main source of transportation for the Chinese people was the bicycle and there were millions upon millions of them. Heavy loads of freight were hauled in a two wheeled wooden wagon pulled by a donkey or a horse, and sometimes even by a woman. The more successful communes had big (what we used to call) 'garden tractors' and the driver of those two wheeled motor driven vehicles would sit on the trailer he was pulling and steer the garden tractor with the handle bars much like a lawn mower.

The Japanese government was ahead of the American government because they began doing business with their once hated enemy long before President Nixon visited China in the mid 70's and opened the doors. Do you remember the term the iron curtain? Regardless of what you thought of President Nixon he had a wonderful talent in breaking the ice to our once sworn enemies, and he did.

Long before Americans ever visited China, Japan made peace with them and seeing that China was determined to become a powerful country the Japanese introduced them to the idea of tourism. They first acquired a contract to sell them modern and air conditioned tour buses. By doing so they also volunteered to provide driver training to selected Chinese garden tractor drivers. Before long the Japanese people were touring China and this occurred just before the Americans finally decided to bury the hatchet and become friendly.

The need for paved roadways became obvious to the Chinese government officials and to accomplish this endeavor they needed multitudes of manpower. We, (some of the first American visitors to China) got to see this road building process in action. You have never seen so many wheel barrows and shovels and tampers in your life. They had huge metal tanks for mixing blacktop and many Chinese workers mixing the hot blacktop (tar and chipped stone). Other workers were shoveling the mixed blacktop into the wheel barrows and the driver of the wheel barrow would push his heavy load to where it needed to be dumped while more Chinese workers raked it out into a smooth layer of hot blacktop. Still more Chinese workers with flat metal tampers on the end of an iron pole were tamping the blacktop into a compacted mass of pavement. They could cover a two lane highway about a half mile per day and they had thousands of miles to go! It one point I mentioned to my local Chinese interpreter that in America we had machines that could do all that work automatically. His response was, "maybe so but look how many people you would make unemployed if we did that". He had a good point!

On yet another occasion I watched as hundreds of strong Chinese men with little more clothing than a pair of pants and a pair of shoes carried on their backs (protected by a hemp mat) huge boulders that must have weighed 150 to 200 pounds each. They were tied up with a length of rope and carried from where the donkey drawn cart dropped them near the river as these men carried them one by one down the bank and loaded then on to a barge. The barge was then towed out to a designated spot on the river and one side of the barge was flooded, causing it to roll on to its side dumping the load of boulders to the bottom. They were building a bridge to span the river and these huge boulders were for the pilings on which the bridge was to be built.

They have advanced their country from the primitive times in the 70's to what today is probably one of the most modern countries in the world. The have accomplished this in a matter of 30 years but I might mention they had the help and guidance of America and of course Japan.

Yes, they indeed were the good old days!

CHAPTER 35

My Greatest Blunders and Some of my Talents

On more than one occasion I have made errors in judgment. Being a guide and tour director did not immune me from making them and I have probably made more than my share.

One of the first lessons I learned was that being a tour director is not, and should not be a representative democracy. I made the mistake of asking for feedback from my group of travel agents on a choice of two different options of places to visit. We were in Japan and in Japan there are allot of shrines and tons of Buddhist temples. They insist that we tourists see them all. I finally succeeded in convincing my local guide in Tokyo that if my group would rather take a boat ride on beautiful Lake Hakoni than to go all the way to Nara to see the world's largest Buddha, inside a building then we would forego the long bullet train ride south. I called a meeting of the group I was directing and posed the question to them of which of the two destinations would they rather see. In my own humble opinion if you see one giant Buddha you have basically seen them all. We have already seen the world's largest Buddha outside a building in Komakura. To see another one just as big but inside a building just did not appeal to me. When you couple what I have just explained, with the fact that there are wild deer roaming around that park in Nara that continue to bite you in the butt until you finally buy some deer treats from the local vendors to feed the nagging deer. You then recognize my suggestion of a pleasurable boat ride on beautiful Lake Hakoni as a more desirable choice. Wrong! I asked the group of 36 travel agents and wouldn't you know it! 18 folks wanted to go to Nara and 18 wanted to go to Lake Hakoni. I was the deciding vote and I chose Lake Hakoni and immediately angered half the group. I would never make that mistake again and I am glad it happened to a group of travel agents and not paying tourists. I knew from then on there would never be any future choices when it came to places to visit! I became a dictator!

I have always had a sense of humor and I used it allot to dispel fears or anxieties. On another of my major blunders I had the opportunity to use humor to dispel the fear of flying in one of my female group members. Now I should explain that when groups of more than 15 people travel together there is a substantial discount on air fares bus fares train fares etc. Consequently we were usually given seat assignments very close to, if not at the very rear of the airplane. We were assembling at the airport in some foreign country when one member of my group asked me why we always had to sit at the very rear of the airplane. Without thinking to deeply about the question I promptly responded saying that the rear of the aircraft was the safest place to sit. When another group member questioned my answer I again responded saying 'well, you never heard of an airplane backing into a mountain have you'? The poor woman with the fear of flying became instantly very ill and puked all over the highly polished floor of the airport lobby. Then as if I did not already feel bad enough for using such poor judgment, the woman insisted on sitting next to me and that I must hold her hand during takeoff and landing. I never realized that a small woman such as she was, had anything close to the amount of strength she had in her right hand! It was about a week later when I finally got the feeling back in my left hand! I never used that joke again!

I strived for perfection! There was nothing more I wanted to do then to keep my groups very happy, secure and safe. I did not want them to have to go through the process of customs and entry procedures in foreign countries or to even have to handle their baggage. I wanted to do all that work for them, and I did. If I met the group in Seattle or anywhere on the west coast of the USA I would always ask for their airline tickets and passports. I carried a brief case and I was always dressed in a suit and tie. I would approach the departure desk and present the air tickets and passports of the entire group, along with the appropriate departure tax in each and every country we visited. From the time we left the USA until they returned they never touched their baggage once. I did it all. Once we departed and were on our way to the Orient or Southeast Asia I did all the legwork. I had large 5X7 colored and water proof tags (all of the same color) attached to every checked bag the group had. Each member was allowed two bags so if I had 36 members in the group I had 72 bags. If 72 bags with color coded tags were checked in when we departed then 72 color coded bags were required when we arrived at each and every country we visited. The only help I ever needed was for 4 or 5 men to help me push the 4 or 5 carts from the baggage claim area to the port of entry once passed the port of entry the airport aides would push the carts behind me as the group followed the carts to be loaded onto the bus or the truck that followed the bus that we took to the hotel. I had literally handled each and every bag from the carrousel to the cart. The hotel staff unloaded the baggage from the bus and delivered it to each and every room. The traveler never had to handle their bags, airline tickets, stand in line to check in or pay departure taxes. I did that all for them.

Sometimes if we were on a long bus ride I would break the monotony by having the group sing songs or I would just use the microphone to entertain the group.

Although I was single I had a "doctored" photograph of what had to be the world's ugliest woman. Sometimes I would catch the group completely off guard by standing up in front of them and with the saddest look on my face ask them how everything was back in the good old USA. I would go into a long conversation about how I missed the USA and my lovely wife. I would usually say I had not been home for months. I could see the sadness and sympathy on their faces and then I would dig out the photo and look lovingly at it and the women usually wanted to see what she looked like. It would usually be just one glance and the entire bus was rolling in laughter! I did this on several occasions but it became too boring even for me so I quit using that type of entertainment. Little by little I learned to be a proficient and entertaining tour director if I must say so myself. I was in demand for my directing skills by most of the international airline carriers for many years.

I would have continued in this career had terrorism not raised its ugly head and created fear in traveler's minds causing a steep decline in group travelers.

Over the years I made many friends throughout the Orient, China and SE Asia not to mention friends scattered throughout the USA.

I hope the day will come when once again group travel can flourish and people can travel and experience the different cultures of the world with no fear of night club bombings or car bombs or snipers firing bullets.

I am so very thankful for the many folks I have had the pleasure of meeting and serving over the years and may all your travels be safe and enjoyable experiences.

CHAPTER 36

Red Lake Today

I have not been to Red Lake since 1957. In 1956 and 57 there was not much in computer technology if any. There was no such thing as "Google Earth". Today we have advanced technology that can show you what areas in 1956 and 1957 look like today from altitude.

When I look at Red Lake and point's North on Google Earth, I hardly recognize anything. There are roads now where there was nothing but wilderness before. Our cabin for instance was the last one from town on what today is called "Goldshore Rd". The wilderness that I used to hike is now crisscrossed with new and paved roads. I was so very fortunate to have lived there when it was still an untamed wilderness.

In 1956 the Town of Red Lake was the end of the road. There was only one road into Red Lake and that road was 113 miles of pure dirt. Any point north of Red Lake had to be reached with a Bush Plane or dog sled and there were an abundance of both of them. There were many privately owned single plane bush pilots as well as two small airlines in Red Lake. One of those airlines was Ontario Central Airlines and that company consisted of 3 single engine Norseman aircraft and two single engine Beaver aircraft. Both of those aircraft are work horses when it comes to bush planes. The company my father flew for had three aircraft. There was a "T" craft airplane which was a small single, 65 HP engine, airplane that could haul a maximum load of around 400 pounds. Then there was a super cub with a single 85 HP single engine and the load capacity for that plane was around 600 pounds. The plane my father flew was a new Cessna 180 single engine aircraft. I think the load capacity of that plane was close to 1000 pounds. All of these planes were configured to haul freight so there was only one seat and that seat was for the pilot. All the rest of the floor space was for freight and the floor was covered with tie down rings. All the bush planes in 1956 and 1957 were equipped with snow skis for landing gear on the lakes in the winter and Pontoons for landing on lakes in the summer time. I do not know when this procedure was changed but I am certain it was not soon after I had left the area of Northwestern Ontario.

When looking at the Google Earth views of Red Lake and points north today it is almost unbelievable the amount of changes that have taken place since my years there. Not only is the town of Red Lake littered with roads going in all directions but there are now roads going north from there and instead of bush planes being equipped with either ski's or pontoons they now have wheels since they have cut air strips at all the villages that were served by bush planes in the past using ski's and pontoons.

I suppose this is progress but I must say I think it had to be more fun in the wild and wooly days of 1956 and 1957 when Saturday night entertainment was picking up drunken Indians and hauling them to the hospital to get patched up.